ANGELIC MYSTERIES

DR. RICKY ROBERTS

ANGELIC MYSTERIES by Ricky Roberts
Published by Creation House
A Strang Company
600 Rinehart Road
Lake Mary, Florida 32746
www.creationhouse.com

Unless otherwise noted, all Scripture quotations are from the King James Version of the Bible.

The translations of the fathers come from public domain or were done by Dr. Ricky Roberts.

Cover design by Terry Clifton

Library of Congress Control Number: 2004109819
International Standard Book Number: 1-59185-630-2

First Edition

05 06 07 08— 98765432
Printed in the United States of America

To all those who still believe in the God of the miraculous

Contents

Introduction

ANGELIC MYSTERIES—THOSE HEAVENLY mysteries that include truths about God, Christ, the Holy Spirit, and especially the mysteries about God's angels—have many voices today. The truth about these mysteries is lost in the midst of much misinformation. It is replaced with fairy-tales and other stories invented by Satan. Please notice that the mysteries about God's angels as His messengers of holiness, justice, judgment, and righteousness are overturned and corrupted. Therefore, the libraries of many pastors are filled with books that do not contain the truth about angels and other heavenly mysteries, but that advance a mixture of both biblical and pagan principles about angels and all other heavenly mysteries found in the spiritual realm. It is very common to find, for example, Christian writers who champion such pagan philosophy as platonism and philoism when it comes to the mysteries about God and angels. Both philosophies understand God and angels as formless beings who cannot enter into the physical realm, and are only types of the same divine force. Even the Reformers were fooled into following many pagan philosophies about angels. They tried, commonly, to explain away unknown incidents of angelic power as nothing at all, or as hallucinations.

How far have we fallen from the truth on these mysteries? Does anyone remember how the angels dealt with man before, and after, the fall? If not, it is time for us to remember.

The first mention of angels in Scripture is Genesis 3:24. In Genesis 3:24, two Cherubim are placed at the east entrance to the Garden of Eden. Their purpose was to protect the entrance. They became the visible representatives of God before the deluge.

The immediate introduction of these Cherubim without any pre-warning shows that the appearances of angels were not strange occurrences. In fact, Jewish tradition and documents show that man talked with God and His angels from the very beginning. Even after the fall, man heard the voice of the Lord, knew that God Himself was walking in the garden wanting face to face communication and fellowship with Him, and knew that the angels who were placed over the Garden of Eden were Cherubim. (See Genesis 3:8–13; 3:24.)

One example of this belief, found in Jewish tradition and documents, is that man was not cut off from the enjoyment of meat dishes. While he was not permitted to slaughter animals to appease his appetite at this time, the angels brought him meat and wine, serving him like attendants. As such, man ate the food of the angels. (See Psalm 78:25; Numbers 11; and Exodus 24:9–11.)

The angels were so involved in the life of man before the fall that the relationship between man and angels has not been repaired to what it was. The only time this relationship will be fully realized and become as it was before the fall is at the Rapture. (See Romans 8:14–17; 1 Corinthians 15:24–28; 1 John 3:1–2; John 14:1–3.)

From the very beginning of man's experience with the angels, there came forth knowledge about angels interwoven in monotheism. From this lofty place, much was known about the angels. In fact, man received knowledge of the spiritual realm from the beginning. This very knowledge was interwoven in monotheism, as portrayed in the Bible. Yet as time continued, knowledge about angels degenerated to the realm of the strange. This is because it has been interwoven with other belief systems, such as animism, polytheism, and pantheism, instead of monotheism as taught in the Bible.

This degeneration is what led to an almost complete failure of men to uncover the mysteries of God's angels. If it were not for the Scriptures, the mysteries of God's angels would be impossible to discover. The mysteries of God's angels are found only in the Scriptures. They can only be known to a greater extent by accepting the Word of God as the final authority. The Word of God is the authority against which all that we know about these mysteries must be judged.

Four chapters deal with the orders of God's angels; two chapters deal with the nature of angels; two chapters deal with the works of angels; and two chapters deal with the common facts about them. Other facts about the spiritual realm will also be given throughout the book.

In this first work on angels, I have not dealt with the angel of the Lord, the rank of God's angels compared to that of the saints, or the angels and the doctrine of judgment. Nor have I expounded greatly upon the Pre-Adamite age and the fall of Satan.

VERBUM IPSE DEUS

Notes on Biblical Texts

All critical editions of the Greek New Testament were consulted when dealing with the New Testament and its doctrine. Both the critical and majority views were considered. The Greek New Testament will be known as the Greek New Testament or the Greek text.

The Hebrew text was consulted when dealing with the Old Testament. It is known as the Masoretic Hebrew text. Within this book, it will be referred to by that name.

The Septuagint was also consulted when dealing with the Old Testament. The Septuagint is a translation of the uncorrupted Hebrew text—Mosaic-Ezraic Hebrew text—and must be considered when studying the Old Testament. In this book it will be referred to as the Greek Septuagint.

Pronunciation Notes

The pronunciation of Greek used in this book is that of modern Greek instead of that derived from Erasmus. Modern Greek more resembles that of ancient Greek than the manner in which Erasmus pronounced Greek. Byzantine scholars pronounced ancient and modern Greek in the same manner. Even before the close of the first century the pronunciation of ancient Greek is also found in modern Greek. In the fifteenth century the Greeks, it is reported, still pronounced the Greek language as Plato, Euripides, and Aristophanes did. Further, papyri refute the Erasmian pronunciation. The vowels and diphthongs, coming from the Alexandrine period and written in Koine Greek, were not pronounced in the same manner as that found in the pronunciation of Erasmus, but in the same manner as found in modern Greek.

The pronunciation of Hebrew used in this book is commonly used throughout colleges that still teach Hebrew. It is almost the universal view on how ancient Hebrew was pronounced.

CHAPTER I

The Orders of God's Angels: The Seraphim

THE MOST POWERFUL angels are the Seraphim. The only place in the Bible that they are mentioned is in Isaiah 6:1–7. This passage of Scripture concerns a vision that Isaiah was given in 748 B.C.

Before we dare to look into the facts about these angels, we would do well to understand the background that sets forth the reason for their visitation, followed by common facts about these angels.

Background of Isaiah 6

The phrase "In the year that king Uzziah died," in Isaiah 6:1 shows that the time of this supernatural manifestation of God's power was when Uzziah had not died, but had been struck down in sickness by a mighty judgment of God. This judgment would ultimately lead to his death. The biblical texts do not see Uzziah as already dead, but still alive. This confirms Isaiah 1:1.

What kind of sickness did God strike Uzziah with as judgment against him? Leprosy. Why? God struck Uzziah with leprosy due to his deplorable act of trying to offer incense upon the altar of burnt offerings. (See 2 Kings 15:5 and 2 Chronicles 26:19–21.) According to Jewish tradition, also noted by Josephus, an earthquake occurred.[1] This caused a great breach to be torn in the temple. This great breach allowed a brilliant ray of sunlight to come forth into the temple. This sunlight fell upon the forehead of Uzziah, and he was struck with leprosy.

In Isaiah 6:1, the Greek Septuagint includes something interesting that the Masoretic Hebrew text does not. The beginning of Isaiah 6:1 from the Greek Septuagint reads, "And it came into a new state of being in the year…" This phrase shows something important. Isaiah's life would change from the moment he saw the vision of the Lord and the Seraphim. The pronoun *it* concerns Isaiah's life, the condition of the Jewish people, and something new that was beginning to take place.

The beginning that was to take place in Isaiah's life was quite good. He was about to become a prophet of the Lord. The beginning that was to take place in the Jewish people was quite bad. God was tired of their rebellion against Him and had concluded in 748 B.C. that their kingdom and city must be destroyed. The result of God's judgment against the Jewish people was the destruction of the kingdom of Judah. (See vv. 9–13.) This destruction began in 605 B.C. and ended in 587 B.C.

The same phrase found in the Greek Septuagint, also in Isaiah 6:1, involves the fact that Isaiah was in total astonishment and bewilderment over the notion that God would appear before him, a deprived sinful human. (See Job 15:16; Romans 6:6, 14, 17, 20; 7:5–6; 6:14; 5:12–21; 8:2; Galatians 3:22.) Isaiah could not believe at first what he was seeing in the vision. He was so amazed and bewildered that God would even appear to him that he became speechless. (See vv. 5–6.) His unworthiness was maximized to the fullest.

The fundamental thought of the Greek verb γίγνομαι (yēgənōmě), as found in the Greek Septuagint, describes something or someone moving into a new state of existence. This Greek verb is used as a *momentary aorist*. The *aorist tense* expresses an instantaneous change in Isaiah's life and in the life of the Jewish people.

The time of this supernatural manifestation of God's power was most fortunate for Isaiah. While still a young man, he experienced a shock which was a crisis in his life. This shock included Uzziah being stricken with leprosy, and Isaiah noticing that God had withdrawn His blessings from the Jewish people. Every aspect of Isaiah's life was changed. His whole life was turned upside down. He had thoughts of anguish. By that time his thoughts were almost completely filled with distress. Yet, there was a glimmer of hope.

While Isaiah was still in distress, there was a religious festival—the Day of Atonement. This happened before the death of Uzziah. Isaiah attended this festival and gave genuine worship to the Lord in the court of the priests, hoping to find an answer.

All Israelites were allowed to enter the court of the priests. They were allowed to enter this court for the laying of hands upon the head of the sacrifice to be slain for the slaying of it; for the waving of some part of it after it had been killed; for seeking the Lord in prayers with weeping, fasting, or rejoicing in worship; and for certain festivals. (See 1 Kings 6:3; 2 Chronicles 3:4; 7:17; 8:12; 15:8; Joel 2:17.) In the code of Maimonides, and the works of Dr. Lightfoot, this fact is mentioned.[2]

Due to this fact, Isaiah, as a worshiper, had a right to be in this court. It was common to find worshipers in this court between the porch, leading into the Holy Place and the Holy of Holies, and the altar of burnt offerings. There were twenty-two cubits (32.26 feet to 40.128 feet) space between each, according to the Babylonian Talmud.[3]

Though Isaiah gave genuine worship unto the Lord God, he was bewildered to see that God had not given him some kind of comfort and a light of hope. What he did see made him sick to his stomach. He saw nothing more than a play—drama, filled with pretense. This confirmed what he had known for a considerable time: the Jewish people had become alienated from God. Undoubtedly, this made Isaiah hang his head in shame. While all of this was true, Isaiah watched curiously, believing that something would occur. Through most of the festival in the temple, he watched between the porch and the altar of burnt offerings, still hoping that God would cause something wonderful to happen. Consequently, his hope was rewarded. He began to feel the presence of God and began to sense that something wonderful and awesome was about to take place. Joy, surprise, amazement, bewilderment, and happiness began to fill his body, soul, and spirit. At that very moment, Isaiah began to see something he knew was not of this world. This astonishing incident the soon appointed prophet beheld in a vision restored his faith.

What did the vision consist of? Briefly, Isaiah saw the Lord sitting on a high and exalted throne with the temple filled with the Lord's glory. Seraphim were standing in a stationary manner, with an attitude of service around about the Lord. Each had six wings. Two wings covered their faces, two wings covered their feet, and the other two wings were used for flight.

Isaiah saw the Seraphim praising and worshiping the Lord. He saw one Seraph go forth from the throne and acquire a hot coal from the altar of burnt-offerings. He touched the lips of the prophet with the hot coal.

The person that Isaiah saw in the vision was none other than the Messenger of the Covenant. Who was the Messenger of the Covenant? He was Christ in His preincarnated state. In these appearances, Christ as God was always seen in His divine form.

Though there was a belief that if a man saw the Lord he would die, the truth was that one could see the Lord and live. (See Exodus 33:18–23; Genesis 32:30–31; Judges 6:21–24; 13:15–25; Isaiah 6:5; and Revelation 1:16–18.)

Exodus 33:18–23 makes it clear that one can see the Lord and live, but not in His full and infinite glory. (See v. 22.) No man would survive that. Paul says that God dwells in the light, which is His full and infinite glory. It is His full and infinite glory that no man can approach, and whom no man has seen or can see as long as He is in that light. (See 1 Timothy 6:16.)

Where did the Lord appear to Isaiah in the vision? The reference to the earth proves that God was appearing in the Holy of Holies. (See Isaiah 6:3, 9–12.) The posts of the doors were open so Isaiah could see the Holy of Holies. He saw that the veils had been pulled back. Consequently, this has clear reference to the earthly temple built by Solomon. There is no indication that Isaiah was transported to the throne room of God.

Isaiah saw the Holy of Holies physically while seeing the Lord and the Seraphim spiritually. The Holy place was opened, and the veils were opened for the Day of Atonement. This day above any other day was the time that the High Priest entered the Holy of Holies. He entered it four times.

During these times the veils had to be pulled back for the entrance of the High Priest to bring incense into the Holy of Holies. The veils stayed pulled back only a moment until the High Priest entered the Holy of Holies. People who were between the porch and the altar of burnt offerings could watch from this place. It was at this time that God gave Isaiah the vision. In essence, the vision only lasted a few moments, but it accomplished its purpose. Between the moment the veils were opened and closed for the High Priest, the vision was completed. The veils were also reopened when the High Priest was ready to come out of the Holy of Holies. Yet, this was not the time of the vision.

When Isaiah saw the Lord sitting on a throne, he saw the contrast between the pygmy throne of Uzziah and the throne of the everlasting God. The Lord's throne is high and lifted up in the temple. It is His throne and not Judah's king that is sovereign. Isaiah also realized the utter helplessness of man apart from God. God's throne alone is supreme and absolute above all.

A distressed and bewildered youth went into the temple, but out of the temple came a changed man called into the prophetic ministry. Through this vision, Isaiah was made ready for his calling to be a prophet. Before this moment, Isaiah was not a prophet.

From the time Isaiah received the vision, he possessed the prophetic gift in its highest form, and a message from God with the power to utter it in the most forcible language. From the time of the vision, Isaiah was uncompromising toward sin of all kinds, and he always denounced it with forcible vengeance.

One who obtained the prophetic office was considered a minister of the Most High God, and of His temple. In essence, whether or not a prophet came from the line of Levi, he was considered a special priest to God. At times he would have access to every part of the house of the Lord, including the Holy Place and the Holy of Holies. (See Lamentations 2:20; Jeremiah 23:11; 26:7; 28:5–6; and Zechariah 7:3.) It was commonly known that a prophet had access on occasion to the sanctified area of the temple, which was from the court of the Israelites to the Holy of Holies. Why? A prophet of the Lord came in the place of God by prophesying. As such, the prophet of the Lord was and is considered the Lord's mouthpiece through whom God can speak.

Facts About the Seraphim

This order of angels is known as Seraphim. The singular form is Seraph, the plural Seraphim. The Hebrew form of Seraphim is שְׂרָפִים (Sərāphēm). It appeared in Numbers 21:6, 8; Isaiah 14:29; and Isaiah 30:6. However, it is connected with the Hebrew noun נָחָשׁ (nākhäsh) and means "serpent." When combining both nouns, the translation can only be "burning serpent." These serpents were called "burning" because of the heat, violent inflammation, and thirst caused by their bites. For this reason, the connotation of the Hebrew form of *Seraphim* is not angels, but refers to the characteristic of the serpent's venom and its effects upon a victim.

The Hebrew form of *Seraphim* is derived from the Hebrew verb שָׂרַף

(säräph). This Hebrew verb means "burning." By this alone, the meaning of the name Seraphim is "burning ones." This is also seen to be the case by comparing the name *Seraphim* with *Sarrapu*, which is the name of the god *Nergal*. Many have concluded that this other name for the god Nergal was derived partly from the belief in Seraphim. This belief about the Seraphim was present before Isaiah saw them in a vision. The word *Sarrapu* means "burning" or "burning heat of the sun." From this, the god Nergal is seen as a god known as "the burning one." The third section of the Book of Enoch 7:1 calls the Seraphim the "flashing Seraphim."

The use of the *pluperfect* tense reveals that Isaiah saw the Seraphim in preparation to worship the Lord God in song and chorus. Seraphim who appeared in the vision were present, and all the Seraphim who could be there were present as well. A true gathering of the angelic hosts was also seen to be occurring by this tense.

The Seraphim left the throne, organized a procession in heaven, and then came back with all other Seraphim who could be brought, worshiping the Lord in genuine reverence and humility. (See Isaiah 6:4.)

A Seraph left this great procession of worshiping the Lord and flew to Isaiah with a glowing coal in his hand from the altar of burnt offerings. (See vv. 6–7.) The Seraph who left the great procession was one of the four Seraphim who had originally appeared around God and His throne.

Notice the contrast of the Seraphim. The Seraphim worshiping the Lord in genuine reverence and humility with no fakery or pretense contrasted with the manner in which the Jewish people had been worshiping the Lord.

The biblical texts using the verb *stand* denote that the Seraphim were not standing with their feet upon the floor of the temple, but were hovering stationary in the air by their wings. As such, they were not flying about, but using their wings to hover around the Lord and His throne in a stationary manner. The hovering of the Seraphim around the Lord and His throne exposes the superiority of the Seraphim over the other orders of God's angels. In other words, the proximity of the Seraphim to the Lord and His throne stresses that the order of the Seraphim is the highest order of God's angels.

The throne mentioned in Isaiah was a portable throne. It was this throne that was also seen in the visions of Ezekiel. (See Ezekiel 1:4–28; 10:1–22.) Isaiah only saw the portable throne. He did not see the chariot formed by the Cherubim and the Ofannim–wheel angels, but Ezekiel saw both the portable throne and the chariot formed by the Cherubim and the Ofannim. (See Psalm 18:10.)

The omission of the angelic-formed chariot is very significant. It brings to light the importance of the Seraphim over the Cherubim and the Ofannim. In essence, the Seraphim are so powerful that the Cherubim and the Ofannim, after carrying the portable throne to the Holy of Holies, were ordered to depart and not even to be in their presence. Undeniably, God's angels are organized to the extent that angels of each order are only allowed to be in the presence of the higher angels on certain occasions. Evidently, this was not a time that the Cherubim and Ofannim were allowed to be present with the Seraphim. Even the Cherubim and the Ofannim are not allowed to be in the presence of each other, except on certain occasions.

Originally, only four Seraphim were present as understood by the context given in Isaiah 6:1–7. Each Seraph represented a different group within the order of the Seraphim. The Seraphim, Cherubim, and Ofannim have four groups within their orders.

Isaiah 6:2 is a description of the four Seraphim who appeared around God and His throne, while Isaiah 6:3 is a description of only two. Each Seraph resided in a different direction from the throne of God. The pronoun *they* in verse two refers to the four Seraphim, while the same pronoun in verse two only refers to two of the Seraphim.

The Seraphim are seen to have six wings. The Seraphim covering their face with two wings expressed their reverence to God and their unworthiness to look upon God. The Seraphim covering their feet with two wings expressed their reverence to the Lord God and their humility.

One Seraph cries to the other and says, "Holy, Holy, Holy is the Lord of Hosts." The reference to the Seraphim reciting the word *holy* three times is a direct reference to the Trinity, united in one divine nature. (See Deuteronomy 6:4.)

The pronoun *other* distinguishes one Seraph from another, as well as the Seraphim from the Lord God. This is especially done to show a sharp contrast between the Lord and the Seraphim. The pronoun *other*, especially in the Greek Septuagint, also means that the first Seraph is higher in rank than the second within the order of Seraphim. This is achieved by each of these two Seraphim being of a different group within the order. This proves that more than one group of Seraphim were present in this vision. Actually, all the groups of Seraphim, namely four, were present in this vision.

The Seraphim are rightly called *angels of fire*. This is understood from the meaning of their name, and from Isaiah 6:6–7. What is the definition of angels of fire? Angels of fire are angels—the Seraphim, Cherubim, and Ofannim—who use two kinds of fire. These fires are spiritual fire and physical fire. The Seraphim use spiritual fire in two specific ways, and physical fire in one. The Cherubim and the Ofannim use spiritual and physical fire in only one specific way.

The Seraphim, Cherubim, and the Ofannim are not determined to be angels of fire by their appearance. All of God's angels can have the appearance of flaming fire. (See Psalm 104:4; Hebrews 1:7; 2 Thessalonians 1:7–9.) Therefore, a fiery appearance does not determine that an angel of God is an angel of fire. What determines this is their work and especially their name. On occasion, other signs are used to signify that an angel is an angel of fire: the appearance of a whirlwind associated with an angel, their connection to the name Seraphim, an ability to change color, and a different name from what they are usually called. Not all these other signs have to be present to distinguish an angel as an angel of fire. One is sufficient.

Physical fire is that kind of fire that can be perceived by the five physical senses (sight, hearing, touch, smell, and taste) and by spiritual means. Spiritual fire is the kind of fire that cannot be perceived by the five physical senses, but only by spiritual means.

Isaiah 6:6–7 describes a Seraph carrying a fiery piece of coal from the altar of burnt offerings in Solomon's temple. This piece of coal touches the mouth of Isaiah and does no harm. What does this show? That the Seraph had the ability to change physical fire so that it would not hurt Isaiah. What kind of fire was it changed into? Spiritual. This indicates that the Seraphim can use and control fire. In addition, it shows that the Seraphim can change the very nature of fire. Further, the Seraphim can call both physical and spiritual fires into existence by the power of God. They can even use and control fire that has already been in existence.

All angels can use and control physical or spiritual fire. (See Isaiah 6:6–7; Ezekiel 10:1–7; Exodus 3:2; Acts 7:30; Judges 6:21; Revelation 8:5; 9:1–21; 14:18.) Still, only angels of fire can use physical fire to bring forth literal judgment as with Sodom and Gomorrah, and they can only use spiritual fire as a sign of impending judgment. The Seraphim are the only ones able to use it as a sign of impending purification. All angels have the power to call both physical and spiritual fires into existence by the power of God just like the Seraphim, Cherubim, and Ofannim. (See Judges 6:21.)

The Seraphim did not purify Isaiah in any way, but they were used to bring forth a sign of purification as found in Old Testament atonement. What was the sign? Spiritual fire.

The purification that Isaiah received from God was a ceremonial purification from his sins, the power of Satan, and spiritual death. In these cases then, the appearance of spiritual fire and the use of it is a sign that God's purification is on its way. The Seraphim used the spiritual fire also in Isaiah 6:1–7 as a sign of impending judgment upon the kingdom of Judah.

Further, spiritual fire is used in a special manner in the underworld. While the underworld is part of the spiritual realm, its location is literally in the heart of the earth (Matt. 12:40), the lower parts of the earth (Eph. 4:8–10), the nether parts of the earth (Ezek. 31:14, 18; 32:18–27), and beneath the earth like a pit (Prov. 15:34; Isa. 14:9–15). The underworld is in the very core of the earth. The spiritual and physical realms occupy the same space within the core of the earth, but different dimensions.

Spiritual fire is the kind of fire that truly torments the wicked in the underworld. It is real fire, not symbolic. It is the kind of fire that torments all fallen angels, all demons, and all the wicked humans.

Physical fire cannot torment a soul, yet spiritual fire can. Physical fire can only be used to torment physical bodies. Spiritual fire can be used to torment disembodied spirits in the underworld and those who have spiritual bodies. The wicked humans in the Second Resurrection will receive human incorruptible and immortal bodies similar to spiritual bodies. From that point on, they will be tormented in them by spiritual fire. (See Daniel 12:3; John 5:28–29; Revelation 20:4–6.) In other words, as with redeemed humanity after the resurrection, they will still have a physical nature though certain parts being like a spiritual nature. One particular part is that their physical bodies are transformed to be like spiritual bodies. However, these bodies will still have flesh and bone. The Greek adjective πνευματικός (pnĕvmātēkōs) in 1 Corinthians 15:44 demands that while angels have spiritual bodies, the resurrected bodies will be similar to theirs.

13

It must be said that spiritual fire is just as real and material in its realm as physical fire is in its realm. It can be seen, touched, smelled, and tasted by spiritual beings. Spiritual fire can also be seen, touched, smelled, and tasted by demons through something that imitates these senses. Being disembodied spirits, they lost these senses.

Are the angels of God and satanic forces tormented now with this fire? God specially created this kind of fire to torment the wicked creatures that rebelled. (See Matthew 25:41.) However, God also created an immunity to this fire. (See Isaiah 6:6–7; Ezekiel 10:1–7; Exodus 3:2; Acts 7:30; Judges 6:21; Isaiah 24:21–22; Revelation 8:5; 9:1–21; 20:1–2, and 14:18.) It is this immunity that God has given to the good angels, so that this fire cannot affect them. God has even given Satan, the fallen angels who are still loose, and demons this immunity. However, God, by His power, will strip this away at the time of final judgment.

It was due to this immunity that the Seraphim could hold and touch spiritual fire without any harm being done to him. This immunity is also present in God and the saints in heaven, and will be present in all the saints.

The Seraphim use physical fire to bring forth literal judgments upon persons, nations, cities, and whatever else God orders. Physical fire was used in this capacity when fire destroyed Sodom and Gomorrah through the ministration of two Cherubim. (See Genesis 19.) The Seraphim cannot be the angels used to destroy Sodom and Gomorrah. The Seraphim have wings and those who were used in the destruction of Sodom and Gomorrah had no wings. The only ones who fit here were the first group of Cherubim since they have no wings.

It is this essential fact that answers the question of why Seraphim means "burning ones." The Seraphim are angels who administer God's wrath and judgment. They, along with the Cherubim and Ofannim, are the ones almost exclusively that execute the judgments. When they execute the judgments of the Lord, these judgments are not limited to those who require physical fire. Why? God's judgments can be executed without physical fire. As such, they execute judgments in a wide range, even today. Not all the judgments that they execute have to do with killing or destruction. Bringing oppression and chastisement are also effective ways to obtain attention and warning.

Studying the many judgments upon people, nations, and cities, as recorded in the Bible, reveals the wide variety of judgments that the Seraphim, Cherubim, and Ofannim mostly execute. Even today, the Seraphim, Cherubim, and Ofannim are used in this way. Other angels only occasionally are used in this capacity.

Spiritual fire is used in several ways:

+ Spiritual fire is used as a sign that the anointing of the Holy Spirit is upon a life. (See Matthew 3:11; Acts 2:3.) Further, spiritual fire symbolizes the Holy Spirit Himself and the rest of the Holy Triune God. (See Deuteronomy 4:24; Acts 2:3; Exodus 9:3; 24:17; Isaiah 33:14; Hebrews 12:29; Lamentations 1:13.)

+ Spiritual fire is used as a sign of revival. (See Acts 2:3.)

+ Spiritual fire is one element that consists of the Lord's Shekinah Presence.

+ Spiritual fire is used as a sign of God's approval, acceptance, mercy, guidance, and protection upon a person, nation, and city. (See Exodus 13:21; 14:24; 24:17, Numbers 14:14; Exodus 3:2; 19:18; Isaiah 6:4; Ezekiel 1:4; Revelation 1:14.)

+ Spiritual fire is used as a sign of God's wrath. (See Daniel 7:10; Deuteronomy 32:22; Isaiah 10:17; Ezekiel 21:3; 2 Thessalonians 1:7–9; Hebrews 12:29; John 3:36; Jeremiah 4:4; 15:14; Ezekiel 22:21, 31; 38:19.)

+ Spiritual fire is used as a sign of impending judgment. (See 2 Thessalonians 1:8.)

+ Spiritual fire is a sign of severe trials, vexations, and misfortunes. (See Zechariah 12:9; Luke 12:49; 1 Corinthians 3:13–15; 1 Peter 4:12.)

+ Spiritual fire is used as a sign of impending purification from sins, the power of Satan, and spiritual death. (See Isaiah 6:1–7.)

+ Spiritual fire is the fire found in the underworld, which torments and will torment in the future all the wicked there.

- Spiritual fire is used as a sign of God's inspiration upon something. (See Psalm 39:3; Jeremiah 20:9.)

- Spiritual fire is used as a sign of possession. (See Acts 2:3.)

- Spiritual fire is used as a sign of God's holiness. (See Exodus 3:2; 19:18; Isaiah 6:4; Ezekiel 1:4; Revelation 1:14; Hebrews 12:29.)

- Spiritual fire is used as a sign of God's healing power. (See Acts 2:3; Numbers 21:6–8.)

- Spiritual fire is used as a sign of God's power. (See Acts 2:3; Revelation 11:15; Deuteronomy 4:24.)

- Spiritual fire is used as a sign of the emblem of the unknown tongues, and those who have been endowed with them. (See Acts 2:3.)

- Spiritual fire is used as a sign of a visitation by God, angel(s), or both. (See Exodus 3:2; 19:18; Ezekiel 1:4; Revelation 1:14; Daniel 7; 10:5–7; Isaiah 6:1–7; Genesis 3:24; Ezekiel 1:4–28.)

Angels often take a small spark of this spiritual fire and place it on a city, nation, or person. This signifies that one or more of the signs are upon it. Only the angels of fire can use it as a sign of impending judgment. Only the Seraphim belonging to the angels of fire can use it as a sign of impending purification. To restate it, in Isaiah's vision, the Seraphim used it to denote both a sign of impending judgment upon Judah, and a sign of impending purification upon Isaiah.

Physical fire is used in a literal sense to destroy and to eradicate the wicked. (See Genesis 19:24; Leviticus 9:24; 10:2; 11:1–3, Numbers 16:35; 26:10, 2 Samuel 6:7; 2 Kings 1:10–14; Jeremiah 43:12.) In other words, it is used as an instrument of destruction. In some incidents, physical fire can symbolize many things that spiritual fire symbolizes. (See 2 Kings 1:10–14; Leviticus 9:24; 1 Kings 18:25.) In these scriptures, physical fire is literally used to burn up the offering and the fat offered to God on the altar. (See Leviticus 9:24, 1 Chronicles 21:36; 2 Chronicles 7:1; 1 Kings 18:25; and the 102 men in 2 Kings 1:10–14.)

The Seraphim of the angelic orders are the least in number in the kingdom of God. The Seraphim and all other of God's angels are seen in Scripture to guard and vindicate the righteousness and the holiness of God (See Isaiah 6:1–7; Genesis 3:24; Exodus 26:1; 35; 36:8) The Seraphim and all of God's angels are associated with the Shekinah Presence. (See Isaiah 6:1–7; Ezekiel 1:4–28; 10:4, 19; 11:22.)

In Isaiah 6:1–7, the appearance of the Seraphim is associated with the prophet Isaiah and his commission. The Seraphim signified that his commission came not from men, but from God.

Chapter 2

The Orders of God's Angels:
The Cherubim

THE CHERUBIM ARE the second most powerful angels. (See Genesis 3:24; Ezekiel 1:4–28; Revelation 4:6–5:14.) The background of Genesis 3:24 will now be discussed.

The Background of Genesis 3:24

The Cherubim, who were of the first group, in Genesis 3:24 guarded the Garden of Eden from the possibility of man entering it. These Cherubim guarded the gate of Eden to allow man entrance only when he had become purified and perfected.

In studying Genesis 3:24, there are three subjects. The first is man, the second is the Cherubim, and the third is the flaming sword. From this, the flaming sword and the two Cherubim are different. The purpose of the Cherubim was to guard the entrance of the Garden of Eden. The purpose of the flaming sword was to protect the Tree of Life from the possibility of men eating fruit from it and becoming immortal deprived human beings. For that reason, the Cherubim and the flaming sword were used by God for two different purposes.

The flaming sword has a spiritual nature, and it is not the nature of angels. It partakes of a spiritual nature the way the spiritual horse-chariots do, as well as other things found in the spiritual realm that are inanimate. This is only one sword of many found in the spiritual realm. Angels can hold swords.

Man was stationed at the outskirts of the Garden of Eden.

The Hebrew verb שָׁכַן (shäkhān) found in Genesis 3:24, from the Masoretic Hebrew text, denotes "To place in a tabernacle." This means that the angels were stationed against the Garden of Eden in a tabernacle. It was this place, which was a local tabernacle, that the Shekinah Presence resided. This was the place that the primeval family came and worshiped the Lord, and where man learned how to worship the Lord. This place continued until the flood destroyed it. (See Genesis 6:1–8:14.) After the flood, the Garden of Eden, the Cherubim, and the flaming sword disappeared.

From Jewish documents, for example, 2 Baruch 4:2–7, the Books of Adam and Eve 25:3, the belief is that as the flood began, God removed the Garden of Eden from the earth and placed it in heaven. With this, the Tree of Life and the Tree of Knowledge of Good and Evil were also taken up from the earth to heaven as part of the Garden of Eden. This must be the case, since no one has ever found the Garden of Eden, the Tree of Life, or the Tree of Knowledge of Good and Evil on earth after the flood.

With the transportation of the Garden of Eden to heaven, there are now two paradises in heaven. The first is Adam's, while the other is God's. The Garden of Eden also can be known as "the earthly paradise." The paradise of God can be known as "the heavenly paradise."

The Garden of Eden will be moved from heaven near to earthly Jerusalem between the Second Coming and the Millennial Reign of the Millennial Kingdom. It is during this time that earthly Jerusalem will be renovated after the pattern of New Jerusalem. (See Revelation 20:9; Daniel 12:11–12; Isaiah 2:2–4; 11:11–12:6; Jeremiah 17:25; 31:38–40; Ezekiel 34:1–35; 40:1–46:24; 43:7; 48; Joel 3:17–20; Micah 4:7; Zechariah 8:3–23; 14:1–21; Revelation 3:12; 4–5; 10; 11:19; 14:17; 16:17; 21:2.)

Irenæus taught that the earthly Jerusalem will go through so much renovation that it will look very much like the heavenly (New) Jerusalem.[1] It will be different from New Jerusalem in three primary ways: it will not have a temple, a paradise, nor one throne each for God the Father and Christ. At this time, the Garden of Eden will once more become the paradise of earth.

In 1 Enoch 25:4–6 and 2 Enoch 8:5, the Garden of Eden is seen to be in heaven until the time between the Second Coming and Millennial Reign of the Millennial Kingdom. (See Daniel 12:11–12.) At this time, it will be transferred from heaven near to earthly Jerusalem and be placed in the Millennial Temple forever. According to the Testament of Levi 18:9–11, at this time the Garden of Eden will be opened to the saints with the sword being removed from it. A throne for God the Father and another throne for Christ will be established in the Millennial Temple near the Garden of Eden. (See Ezekiel 43:7.) According to Isaiah 2:2–4 and 35:8, Micah 4:1–4, and Ezekiel 37:26 and 45:1–5, the Millennial Temple will be set apart from earthly Jerusalem and be placed in the midst of the Holy Oblation. The Garden of Eden will be found in this Millennial Temple.

There is a paradise in heaven, proven by 2 Corinthians 12:1–4 where Paul was caught up into that place. Actually, paradise is found in the part of heaven known as New Jerusalem. Christ mentions this paradise in Revelation 2:7. According to 2 Enoch 8:3–5, 40:2, and 65:10, the Testament of Dan 5:12, 2 Enoch 65:10, 4 Ezra 4:7–8, 5:52, 7:23, and 8:20, the heavenly paradise is the prototype of the Garden of Eden. In addition, in Revelation 22:2, many Trees of Life are mentioned as found in the heavenly paradise in New Jerusalem. According to Jewish sources cited above, the Tree of Life found in the Garden of Eden was an offspring of the original Tree of Life found in the heavenly paradise. The original Tree of Life is of ineffable goodness and fragrance, and is adorned more than every other Tree of Life. It is formed of gold and vermilion and is covered by fire. Therefore, there are many Trees of Life.

There are four paradises mentioned in Scripture. The first one is Lucifer's. (See Ezekiel 28:11–19.) The second one is the Garden of Eden. (See Genesis 2:8–3:24.) The third one is in heaven. (2 Corinthians 12:1–4; Revelation 2:7; 14; 22:2.) The final one is found in the underworld, which is now empty. (See Ephesians 4:8–11; Hebrews 2:14–15; Luke 16:25.)

Facts About the Cherubim

The name of these angels is Cherubim. The singular form is Cherub, while the plural is Cherubim. The Hebrew form of Cherubim is כְּרֻבִים (kərūvēm) in the plural. The meaning of Cherubim is connected to the name Seraphim. Therefore, the name *Cherubim* means "burning ones."

This meaning connects the Cherubim to the name *Seraphim*, and shows that they are angels of fire.

A form of the name *Cherubim* is found in Egyptian writing. This form is Cheresu, and its meaning is "burning ones." To the Jews, the name *Cherubim* was derived from the Hebrew verb חָרוּך (khärūkh). It means "burned" and "scorched." From this, the meaning of Cherubim was seen to be the "burning or scorching ones." This new element of the Cherubim, in their name, identifies that angels of fire are scorching ones. Why? Because they can, and the Cherubim do quite often, when using physical fire to bring forth literal judgment, scorch lands. (See Genesis 19.)

In 3 Enoch 2:1, it calls the *Cherubim* the "cherubim of devouring fire." This name is given to the Cherubim because they are angels of fire. In 3 Enoch 7:1, the Cherubim are called "the blazing Cherubim" for the same reason.

The Cherubim are also called "living creatures" (Ezekiel 1:5; 3:13; 9:1–10:15; 13–15; 17; 19–22; 20; Revelation 4:6, 8, 9.) The name *living creatures* is derived from the plural Hebrew noun חַיָּה (khīyäh) and this plural Hebrew noun literally means "living ones." The living creatures in the Book of Revelation are Cherubim. Why? The Greek noun ζῶον (zōōn) is used to describe the spiritual beings in Ezekiel, from the Greek Septuagint, and in Revelation. Evidently, John used this Greek noun to reveal that there was a connection between the spiritual beings found in the Book of Revelation and those found in the Book of Ezekiel. The connection is that they are the same—Cherubim.

In Ezekiel 28:14, Lucifer is described as a Cherub. It is noteworthy to look at how the Greek Septuagint confirms this fact. The beginning part of Ezekiel 28:14 states that from his beginning, Lucifer was with the Cherubim. The word *cherub* denotes that a singular number is used here. The word *cherub* is understood here to denote commonly the order of the Cherubim, and denotes in specific terms the Cherubim of the first group to which Lucifer belonged. This group is the most powerful of the Cherubim. The Greek preposition μετά (mĕtä) being used with the *genitive of relationship* denotes that Lucifer:

- had the same origin, existence, and beginning as all other Cherubim.

- is associated with, and belongs to, the first group of Cherubim.

22

The first group of Cherubim is seen in Ezekiel 9:1–11 where Ezekiel beholds six Cherubim going about executing God's judgment upon Jerusalem. In a vision, Ezekiel beholds Cherubim acting out before him what would befall Jerusalem because of the wickedness committed. This would come about shortly. They would be the principal reason the Babylonian empire would conquer Jerusalem and what remained of the kingdom of Judah. The Babylonian empire was going to receive angelic help in this endeavor.

The seventh Cherubim angel's task was to place a mark upon the foreheads of those who were God's people in Jerusalem. The appearance of this angel was a sign to Ezekiel that this angel would go about marking those who were of the Lord during the actual destruction of Jerusalem so that they would be saved.

In this vision, Ezekiel saw in his mind a drama, an act, or play of the future, which would befall Jerusalem because of the rebellious attitude of the Jewish people. The angels in this drama played out their parts to perfection, which in reality would occur again. However, any part that Ezekiel had in the vision or anything done for the sake of Ezekiel in his understanding would not literally take place again.

The six Cherubim angels came from the north as did the Cherubim and the Ofannim in Ezekiel 1 and 10.

How is it known that these six angels are Cherubim and part of their first group? It is known that these cherubim are of the first group due to their appearance as men and action.

In Ezekiel 1:4–28, 3:13, 10, and 11:20, both the Cherubim and the Ofannim are associated with the prophet Ezekiel and his commission. The Cherubim and the Ofannim were used to signify that his commission came not from men, but from God. The appearance of the Cherubim and the Ofannim along with the Lord is a supernatural emblem of God's approval of and commission of Ezekiel as a prophet of the Lord God. Ezekiel was commissioned to be a prophet before the Jews who were in rebellion against God.

In 598 b.c., under the third expedition by Nebuchadnezzar, Ezekiel was taken prisoner along with Jehoiachin and others. He was the son of a Zadokite priest. Because of this, he was a priest and of the tribe of Levi. He became both a priest and prophet. When he became a prophet he did not cease being a priest, but God used him in both capacities.

Skeptics will point out that in the Greek Septuagint, the Greek name Ἰωακείμ (Yōākēm) is the Greek form of the name Jehoiakim, and as such has no reference to King Jehoiachin. However, this Greek name in 2 Kings 24:6 makes references to both King Jehoiakim and King Jehoiachin. Accordingly, the Greek name Ἰωακείμ (Yōākēm) can be used for King Jehoiakim or King Jehoiachin. In Ezekiel 1:2, there is a reference to Jehoiachin.

Ezekiel was in his thirtieth year when his ministry as a priest and a prophet began. He lived in a town on the Chebar in Babylonia, a canal that flowed from the Euphrates. It is very well established that to the east of the great city of Babylon, in a territory closely connected with its canals, Nebuchadnezzar established a community of Jews having the best elements of the Jewish race, including political, economic, social, religious, and militaristic leaders. (See Ezekiel 1:3; 12–14; 17:3–6.) His call and commission to the great office of a prophet occurred in Ezekiel 1:5.

His ministry as a prophet was to remind the exiles of their sins, to bring encouragement to them about their situation, and to counsel his people. It was also to warn them in the face of opposition and persecution. Ezekiel also felt that God had called him to be a watchman for his people to warn them of every danger that threatened them. His responsibility to them only ceased when he had tried everything possible to impress upon them the divine message from God so that they could repent. Ezekiel, like Jeremiah, only saw opposition and skepticism for his efforts.

The very first supernatural manifestation that he experienced was the vision of the Cherubim in 593 B.C. at his commission. (See Ezekiel 1:4–28.) In this vision, he was transported from Babylonia to the temple in the spirit. (See Ezekiel 8, 9, and 10.) These Cherubim, who were of another group from those who are mentioned in Genesis 3:24, Ezekiel 9:1–11, and 28:14, were accompanied with the Ofannim. God used the Cherubim and the Ofannim, in this instance, to form an angelic chariot, whose task it was to carry the divine person on the throne to earth and back to heaven or anywhere the divine person wanted to go. Isaiah, in 748 B.C., saw this throne, though the chariot formed by the Cherubim and the Ofannim had already departed by the time Isaiah was allowed to behold that great supernatural manifestation of God's power. The very absence of the Cherubim and Ofannim in the vision of the Seraphim designates that the Seraphim are superior to both of them.

The order of the portable throne and the angelic-formed chariot was this: the divine person was upon the throne with the throne resting upon the Cherubim, and then the Cherubim resting upon the Ofannim. Accordingly, the Ofannim were not only the foundation of the angelic-formed chariot, but also upon which the portable throne of God was and is set.

This is concluded not only from several scriptures in Ezekiel 1 and Ezekiel 10, but especially from Ezekiel 10:2. There the Lord told the man clothed with the long robe to go between the wheels that are under the Cherubim. Ezekiel 10:6 gives more details than Ezekiel 10:2. He states that one Cherub stretched forth his hand into the midst of the fire that was between the Cherubim and the Ofannim, took it, and put it into the hand of the man clothed with the long robe. The fire that was between the Cherubim and the Ofannim was from the altar of burnt offerings in the temple. This shows that the portable throne in this instance was over or above the altar of the burnt offerings.

From Ezekiel 1:15–21 and 10:9–17, it can easily be concluded that during these visions, the portable throne at times was without the angelic-formed chariot, though the four Cherubim and the four Ofannim were still present.

The visions found in Ezekiel 1 to 19 were given to Ezekiel in 593 B.C., four years before the siege of Jerusalem began.

The appearance of the portable throne in Ezekiel 1:4–28 and Ezekiel 10 in the midst of God's judgments infers that God controls His judgments and that the whole flows as a necessary consequence to His holiness. (See Ezekiel 1:22–26; 9; 10:1.)

The Masoretic Hebrew text mentions that the appearance of the Cherubim in Ezekiel 1 and Ezekiel 10 was like burning coals of fire, and like the appearance of lamps. (See Ezekiel 1:13.) However, the Greek Septuagint says that in the midst of the Cherubim, there was the appearance as of burning coals of fire and as the appearance of lamps turning among the Cherubim. The Shekinah Presence was what had the appearance of burning coals of fire and as lamps turning among the Cherubim. The lamps are fires that emitted sparks and flashes of light the way torches do.

The Cherubim and the Ofannim are seen in Ezekiel 1:4–28 and 10:11, with other passages in Ezekiel 10 to be connected with the Cherubim being the leader and the Ofannim doing the following. This is seen from Ezekiel 1:19.

When the Cherubim went, the Ofannim went along with them; and when the Cherubim were lifted up from the earth, the Ofannim were lifted up. This indicates that the Cherubim are higher than the Ofannim in rank, with the Ofannim being directly under the Cherubim's order. Then, Ezekiel 1:4–28 and chapter 10 show that the Cherubim are the second order of angels, and the Ofannim the third order. This inferiority of the Ofannim to the Cherubim is that of rank, not nature.

In Ezekiel 10, the Cherubim are shown to be angels of fire by gathering fiery coals and casting them upon Jerusalem to punish Israel. This was a sign of the impending judgment upon Jerusalem and what remained of the kingdom of Judah. In other words, filling the angel's hand with the coals of fire means that the wrath of God was about to burn the city. (See Ezekiel 10:2.) Taking the coals of fire from the altar of burnt offering shows that God's judgment extended to the earthly temple built by Solomon. It was a Cherubim angel clothed with linen going to the altar of burnt offerings in the temple built by Solomon that took the coals of fire and scattered them about the city of Jerusalem.

Isaiah was a prophet of the kingdom of Judah before the Babylonian captivity. Ezekiel was a prophet of the Most High God when the Babylonian captivity was in process. In 598 B.C., the remaining parts of the kingdom of Judah were going to be brought into judgment by God by the Babylonians. This was completely fulfilled in 587 B.C.

The appearance of the Cherubim and Ofannim uncover the awful state of sin and depravity that was found in the whole generation of Jews. It also reveals the dire consequences that they faced for rebelling against their Creator. Though the Jews deserved to be exterminated completely, God's mercy overrode this thought. Though judgment came, a remnant of a remnant was saved, according to Ezekiel 7:16–22. This reaffirms what the Lord, in Isaiah 6:9, revealed to Isaiah.

From the appearance of the whirlwind in Ezekiel 1:4, the vision of Ezekiel 1:4–28, judgment was on its way against the Jewish nation because of the continual sins that they committed. A whirlwind is an emblem of God's judgment coming upon wicked people and disobedient saints because of their rebellion against Him. (See Jeremiah 23:19; 25:32; 30:23; Isaiah 17:13; 40:24; 41:16.)

The appearance of the Cherubim and the Ofannim in this judgment-vision testifies that they, with the six cherubim of Ezekiel 9, were to be involved in the destruction of Jerusalem and the other remaining parts of the kingdom of Judah. Due to this, they were to help the Babylonians in this task. It is curious that the texts say that this whirlwind came from the north. (See Ezekiel 1:4.) This means that God's judgment would come from the north of Palestine. The Cherubim and Ofannim angels would come from the north, along with the armies of the Babylonians. On this account, the kingdom of Judah would not only be fighting against the armies of the Babylonian empire—physical foes—but also against spiritual foes. Consequently, their efforts were useless and futile. For though they can win against men, they could not win against the supernatural power of Almighty God being manifested through the Cherubim and the Ofannim. No wonder the Jewish people lost! The Jews' constant rebellion against God caused Him to become angry and release His great wrath in a tangible and physical form: "It is a fearful thing to fall into the hands of the living God" (Hebrews 10:31.) Even today, it is a very good thing to fear the Lord God. (See Matthew 10:28; Romans 3:18; 2 Corinthians 7:1; Acts 9:31.)

It is a fact that the holy angels of God who watch over and minister to the saints of God are often employed as the executioners of His vengeance on hypocrites, disobedient saints, and the enemies of the church. That God, from His mercy-seat between the Cherubim, is a consuming fire to all those who despise His great salvation, and His most severe judgments will fall on those who abuse His privileges and are emboldened in their crimes by His patience and mercy. On the other hand, the angels of God penetrate the realms of air, encamp about those who fear him, and protect them from Satan and his forces to whom they would otherwise succumb. (See Psalm 34:7.)

The Cherubim who appeared in Ezekiel 1:4–28 and the same ones in Ezekiel 10 are seen also as eternal reminders of the blessed earthly ministry of the Lord Jesus Christ. Each have four particular faces: lion (chief of the wild animals), ox (chief of the tame animals), man (the head of all), and eagle (chief of the birds). Matthew pictures Christ as a lion, the Messiah. Mark pictures Christ as an Ox, the servant. Luke pictures Christ as the perfect man. John pictures Christ as the Eagle, the Mighty God.

The group of Cherubim who appeared in Ezekiel 1:4–28 and Ezekiel

10 are seen as spiritual beings composed of a mixture of elements. These include having four faces—man in front, right side lion, left side ox, and eagle on the back—on one neck, four wings having two feet like a calf's from which sparks come out caused by the two small wings attached to their ankles, two straight legs having four hands like a man's, and having four sides so that these Cherubim did not have to turn to change direction, but rather could go in any direction the Holy Spirit directed. (See Ezekiel 1:12.)

With two wings they covered their bodies, with the other two they spread out on a level with the head and shoulders and were joined to the edge of the Cherub so that they formed a canopy. In this manner, they soared through the air rather than flew, without any motion of their wings occurring. It is apparent from this that the wings made a great noise when soaring through the air. (See Ezekiel 1:4–28.) When not being part of the angelic-formed chariot, their wings have mobility. They can also move back and forth—clapping or flapping— as seen in Ezekiel 10:5 and Ezekiel 1:24. Truly, the sound of their wings flapping back and forth was heard in the temple from as far as the outer court when they were not part of the angelic-formed chariot.

The Masoretic Hebrew text states that the Cherubim had the very appearance of man in Ezekiel 1:5. From the description given, it is difficult to understand how the Cherubim in Ezekiel 1 and 10 had the appearance of a man. The Greek Septuagint helps in understanding what is truly meant in Ezekiel 1:5. It does not say that the Cherubim mentioned in Ezekiel 1 and 10 had the very appearance of a man, but that the appearance of a man was constantly upon them. The shadow of a man was upon the four Cherubim at once. The shadow was not just upon one of them, but over all of them at once. Whose shadow was upon them? Undoubtedly, it was the Lord's shadow that was upon them all. (See Ezekiel 31:17; Lamentations 4:20; Psalms 57:1; 63; 7; 91:7.) This shadow resembled the appearance of a man. God was sitting upon the throne, as mentioned in Ezekiel 1:26. The fire and light caused the shadow of the Lord. (See Ezekiel 1:4; 1:26–28.)

The Greek Septuagint states that the Cherubim in Ezekiel 1 and 10 have winged feet. (See Ezekiel 1:7.) This text reveals that while the Cherubim had four large wings, they also had winged feet. These wings are not counted among the four wings since these wings are small and joined to the ankle, and not larger than the others. Even the Seraphim have not winged feet, but wings that covered their feet.

The Greek Septuagint states in Ezekiel 1:7 that from the winged feet of each Cherub came sparks. From this, it is a known fact that the wings on the ankles of the Cherubim emitted sparks and flashes of light. This may be like a piece of metal emitting sparks when scraping the highway. According to the Greek Septuagint, the Cherubim's wings are light in weight, yet strong and durable.

Ezekiel 1:9–12 states that the Cherubim in Ezekiel 1 and 10 did not turn to go where the Holy Spirit led them, but they went straightforward. For that reason, when changing directions, they did not have to turn, but went straight in that direction. They had a face looking to each of the four corners of heaven. The symbol here expressed by this supernatural characteristic of the Cherubim is that they made no mistakes, and their work did not need to be redone concerning the judgment that they executed upon the kingdom of Judah. In other words, each went in the direction of the face, which was toward its direction. In whatever direction the Cherubim were to go, they moved forward, since they had faces in every direction.

Ezekiel 1 and Ezekiel 10 uncover the very fact that both the Cherubim and the Ofannim are used to aid in the administration of God's kingdom. Cherubim often symbolize the mercy of God. (See Exodus 25:22; 37:9.) This underscores that God's wrath is almost always intertwined with His mercy.

Both the Cherubim and the Ofannim are seen by Ezekiel 1:4–28 and Ezekiel 10 as the supporters of the divine portable throne and the executors of God's will. All the angels of God are the executors of His will.

In the Book of Revelation, another group of the Cherubim is seen who have six wings and engage in acts of worship. (See Revelation 4–6.) The reference to the Cherubim reciting the word *Holy* three times is a direct reference to the Triune God united in one divine nature. (See Deuteronomy 6:4.)

The group of Cherubim mentioned in Ezekiel 1:4–28 and Ezekiel 10 are often concluded by Ezekiel 1:18 and Ezekiel 10:12 to have many eyes in front and behind. Still, is this true? No! Ezekiel 1:18 and Ezekiel 10:12 make no reference to the Cherubim being full of eyes, but to the Ofannim being full of eyes. In other words, it is the Ofannim who have this characteristic and not this group of Cherubim. There is a group of

Cherubim that has this characteristic and that group is mentioned in the Book of Revelation. (See Revelation 4–6.) This is understood by the Greek Septuagint.

From the name of these angels, the appearance of a whirlwind associated with them, gathering fiery coals and casting them upon Jerusalem, recorded in Ezekiel 10, and their connection to the name Seraphim, the Cherubim are rightly called by the Jews of old "angels of fire." The Cherubim, like the Ofannim, use both the spiritual fire and physical fire in only a specific manner, and that is only for literal judgment.

Ezekiel 10:1–7 describes a Cherub using spiritual fire as a sign that literal judgment is on its way. Genesis 19 depicts that the Cherubim were used in literal judgment scorching the cities and the lands. Both the Cherubim and the Ofannim use spiritual fire as a sign that literal judgment is to follow.

Both the Cherubim and the Ofannim use physical fire to bring forth literal judgment upon persons, nations, and cities. They use this fire to destroy and eradicate uncleanliness and refuse. Not all literal judgments coming from angels of fire are brought forth by physical fire, as already noted. Therefore, both the Cherubim and the Ofannim are angels of fire who execute judgments for the Lord, though also accomplishing many other things for the Lord.

Besides the four Cherubim in Ezekiel 1 and 10, being four literal Cherubim used by God to form the angelic chariot with the Ofannim, they also symbolize that the Cherubim, like the Seraphim, exist in four groups within the order of the Cherubim. This is also seen in Revelation where the four living creatures not only refer to four literal Cherubim, but also the four groups within the order of the Cherubim.

CHAPTER 3

The Orders of God's Angels: The Ofannim

THE OFANNIM, OR wheel-angels, are the third most powerful angels. They are only mentioned in Ezekiel 1:16–21, 3:13, and 10:2–19.

Facts About the Ofannim

The Ofannim are the most curious beings that God created. Ezekiel describes them as having the appearance of a wheel. (See Ezekiel 1:16–21; 3:13; 10:2–19.) However, they are not lifeless wheels at all. They are living wheels with intelligence and other attributes that prove that they are angels. Why would God create angels as this? God sought the best design that He could have for mobility. In other words, God sought to design and create them this way so that they could have complete mobility. Therefore, these angels are the fastest and most mobile of all God's angels.

The name of these angels is Ofannim. The singular form is Ofan while the plural is Ofannim. The Hebrew form of Cherubim is אוֹפַנִּים (ōfánnēm). The other name for these angels is wheel-angels. This is taken from the meaning of this Hebrew noun, which means wheels. The etymology of the name *Ofannim* is the "revolving burning ones." To the Jews, the Hebrew noun אוֹפַנִּים was derived first from the Hebrew verb אָפַן (äfän) and from the Hebrew noun אוֹפִיר (ōfēr). The Hebrew verb root meaning is "revolve."

The Hebrew noun commonly means "gold," but the Jews took it here to mean "burning." Why? The Jews understood that the gold referred to here is of a burning color. From these two words, the Jews concluded that the Ofannim were the third rank of the angels of fire, and became known as the "revolving burning ones." From these very words, they also understood that these angels are angels of fire that can revolve and rotate.

Third Enoch 2:1 calls the Ofannim the "flaming Ofannim." The Jews saw the Ofannim as angels of fire. In 3 Enoch 7:1, the Ofannim are called the "smoldering Ofannim" for the same reason. The Ofannim, besides, are called "Gelgel" in Ezekiel 10:13.

The first picture of the Ofannim involved in the visions of God was in Ezekiel 1:15. The description of the Ofannim is seen as the very appearance of a wheel. Ezekiel saw these angels at first in a stationary position on the earth with each being near one of the four Cherubim. This shows that the portable throne had landed on the ground, and the Cherubim and the Ofannim were no longer stationed below. Why? If they were still carrying the throne, they would have appeared under it since they form the angelic chariot for the throne. The same thing also occurred in Ezekiel 10:9.

The singular number of the Ofannim being used in Ezekiel 1:15 is a direct reference to their unity in forming the angelic chariot for the portable throne of the Most High God. For this reason, the phrase "one wheel" is a collective expression indicating that all four of the Ofannim were, and even now are, united in this duty for the Most High God. In addition, the "one wheel" expresses unity of nature. The four wheel-angels, like all other angels, share the same angelic nature the others have. The difference among angels is due to individuality. Individuality defines whether one is a Seraph, Cherub, Ofan, or another kind of angel. It shows each exists separately and distinctly from any other.

Ezekiel 10:9 shows that the one wheel in Ezekiel 1:15 is a collective expression referring to all four of the Ofannim with one Ofan by each Cherub. The common mistake about the adjective *one* used in the Greek, Hebrew, and Aramaic languages is that many believe it cannot be used as a composite one. However, it can be used as such. (See Genesis 2:24; 11:6; 41:1, 5, 25; 1 Kings 22:13; John 17:22; Acts 4:32; 1 Corinthians 3:8; Exodus 24:3; Numbers 13:23; 14:15; Ezra 3:1; Jeremiah 34:10; Exodus 8:6; 2 Peter 3:8.)

In the Greek Septuagint, the Ofannim are seen as having a golden yellow color and having a dark, burning, fiery red color. This is seen from Ezekiel 1:16 compared to Ezekiel 10:9. Why? The color red is an emblem of God's holy judgment that is to follow. Undeniably, the ordinary color of the Ofannim is a golden yellow color. Nevertheless, when the time that judgment from God must be brought forth is near, their color turns into a dark, burning, fiery red. This red coloring of the Ofannim continues until the judgment ends. When it is over, they change back to their golden yellow color.

From the texts, and how they were written, the appearance of the Ofannim is surrounded in the midst of secrecy. The texts give the best description that can be given about these mysterious beings. The texts say that they are best described as a wheel in the midst of a wheel. To Ezekiel, the Ofannim were surrounded in mystery. He could not see completely the Ofannim. This was due to the Ofannim residing in the Shekinah Presence. The use of the *subjunctive* and *optative moods* by Ezekiel suggest that Ezekiel was completely seized with wonder and bewilderment about the Ofannim. Words could not describe them; yet, Ezekiel only had words.

Ezekiel 1:16 describes the perplexed and puzzled state of Ezekiel. He is seen to have been more perplexed and puzzled in this vision than the second vision. The *optative mood* is used in the first vision, and then the *subjunctive mood* is used in the second vision. This change of mood indicates very well a change of thought in the mind of Ezekiel.

Each of the Ofannim had four sides, or rims, in Ezekiel 1:17 and Ezekiel 10:11. Because each of the Ofannim have four sides and their appearance is best described as a wheel within a wheel, the Ofannim can go any direction without turning. (See Ezekiel 1:17.) This verse has nothing to do with the angelic-formed chariot. Their own appearance is here emphasized.

Ezekiel 1:18 states that their backs turned not as they went. This verse from the Greek Septuagint says that on each Ofan something was placed. But what? The Greek noun ὕψος (ēpsōs) literally means "crown." From this Greek noun, it is seen that the very Shekinah Presence was upon them all as a crown. No wonder it was hard for Ezekiel to describe their action and their appearance!

Ezekiel 1:19 from the Greek Septuagint does not state that the rims of the Ofannim were full of eyes, but their hubs, or the center part of the Ofannim, was full of eyes.

In the second vision of God's portable throne and the angelic-formed chariot, Ezekiel is about to see the Ofannim better and more exact. In this second instance, Ezekiel 10:12 sees that the backs, hands, wings, and the wheels of the Ofannim are full of eyes. The noun *backs* concerns the hubs of wheels, that is, the center part of wheels. Ezekiel saw that the hubs of the Ofannim were full of eyes. (See Ezekiel 1:19.) The noun *hands* deals with the spokes of the wheels. The spokes are seen also to be full of eyes. The noun *wings* concerns the tongues of the wheels, not their wings. From this, the Ofannim are seen to be able to speak. Figuratively, the eyes upon their tongues and lips are a sign that what they said came from the Lord, and their speech was full of intelligence.

In Ezekiel 3:13, Ezekiel records that the Ofannim were able to produce sound. From the Greek Septuagint, the Greek noun φωνὴ (fōnē) means "speech." Ezekiel saw before him, in the vision state, the Ofannim speaking unspeakable words of God's greatness and holiness. That these words were unspeakable words of God is seen by Ezekiel only alluding to them so lightly. Remember what Paul said about unspeakable words in 2 Corinthians 12:1–4?

Ezekiel 3:13 was mentioned for the main purpose to bear witness that the Ofannim have the very ability to speak. Their speech projected a roaring noise throughout the area where they were at, and the sound of their speech covered them as wings. This sound of their speech would echo four times. Each word and its sound would echo through their four rims.

The noun *wheels* deals with the rims of the Ofannim.

The eyes of the Ofannim are real. Figuratively, however, they represent the intelligence of the Ofannim, and their ability to see everything so that nothing can hide from them in doing God's will.

Ezekiel 10:11 expresses that the Ofannim did not turn when they went, but went forward. Since each Ofan is described as having four sides, then each does not have to turn to go in a particular direction, but only has to go forward like the Cherubim mentioned in Ezekiel 1 and 10.

While the way the Ofannim traveled in the visions is described as stationary, the Ofannim are seen to rotate and revolve at very fast speeds. (See Ezekiel 1:15; 10:9.) The Ofannim have the ability to move from a vertical stance to a horizontal stance. Consequently, their rotating and revolving can be done vertically or horizontally. When the Ofannim were stationary, Ezekiel saw them rotating and revolving horizontally. When rotating and revolving, their center is stationary, like a merry-go-round or a carousel.

From the appearance of the whirlwind in Ezekiel 1:4 associated with the Ofannim, their actions, their ability to change color, their name *Ofannim*, and their name *Gelgel*, the conclusion is that the Ofannim are angels of fire.

In the Greek Septuagint, the noun *wheel* comes from the Greek noun τροχος (trōkhōs). This Greek noun has reference also to a very ancient defensive weapon in ancient wars and battles. That weapon is the rotating wheel. This wheel was used in a defensive manner to defend against missile weapons. Could there be a connection to this with the Ofannim? It is believed so! The Ofannim's specialty in both spiritual and physical battles is defensive warfare. Their purpose in the judgment of God upon the kingdom of Judah was to protect and to defend the Babylonians from the rebellious Jews. Often, these angels have been used to defend the Jews, but here they were used to defend their enemies.

In the Christian's warfare against the evil world, Ephesians 6:16 expresses that the shield of faith is used to quench the fiery darts of Satan and his forces. Still, in times of great persecution brought forth by Satan and his forces, the shield of faith will need to be supplemented by angelic help and in a defensive pattern. No angel can be used better than the Ofannim.

The *all* in Ephesians 6:16 as found in translations comes from the Greek adjective πᾶς (päs). Without the article before it, it can only denote a considerable amount. Therefore, it must mean that the shield of faith would quench or stop only a considerable amount. Commonly, it is the gift of faith (see 1 Corinthians 12–13), the shield or hedge of protection (see Job 1:10; 3:23), and the Ofannim or other angels protecting and defending against the fiery darts that the shield of faith cannot handle.

The Masoretic Hebrew text in Ezekiel 10:14 states that the Ofannim had four faces: the first face was the face of a Cherub, the second face was that of a man, the third was that of a lion, and the fourth the face of an eagle. This is baffling. The Greek Septuagint does not have this reference.

In Ezekiel's hearing, the Ofannim were called Gelgel according to the Greek Septuagint. What does Gelgel mean? Gelgel is transliterated from the Hebrew noun גַּלְגַּל (gälgäl). This Hebrew noun means "whirlwind." This proves beyond any doubt that the Ofannim are part of the angels of fire. For "whirlwind," as already said, symbolizes judgment from the Lord. (See Jeremiah 23:19; 25:32; Isaiah 17:13; 40:24; 41:16; Jeremiah 30:23.) Therefore, the Ofannim are angels of fire who especially execute judgments for the Lord.

The Ofannim are closely associated with the Seraphim and Cherubim in ruling God's kingdom in His behalf. This type of angel has a mixture of attributes found in the Seraphim and Cherubim. For this reason, they are very closely connected to each other.

Besides the four Ofannim in Ezekiel 1 and Ezekiel 10 being four literal Ofannim used by God to form the angelic-formed chariot along with the Cherubim, they also symbolize that the Ofannim, like the Cherubim, have four groups within the order of the Ofannim.

In most scholars' lists of angels, the Ofannim are completely ignored. However, the Jews have recognized their existence for many years. In the Babylonian Talmud, the Jews make mention of these angels.[1] It states that these angels are angels of fire. This order of angels is discussed in other Jewish works: 2 Enoch 20:1–3; 29:1–3; 1 Enoch 71:1–17; 3 Enoch 2:1; 6:1–3; 7:1; 19:2–7; 25:1–5, and 33:1–5. In the Dead Sea scrolls, one very interesting document has been found on angels, and it is known as *Litany of the Angels*. In this document, the Ofannim and the Cherubim are mentioned. Consequently, the belief that the Ofannim are angels is very old and is not a modern belief.

CHAPTER 4

The Other Orders of God's Angels

Angelic Riders

THE ANGELIC RIDERS, who ride on supernatural horses and in supernatural chariots, are the fourth most powerful angels. (See 2 Kings 2:11–12; 6:13–17; Zechariah 1:7–21; 6:1–8.) They can also be called "horsemen" and "chariot-drivers."

Facts About These Angels

In 2 Kings 2:11–12, the event of Elijah's translation from the earth to heaven is described. He is translated to heaven by a chariot of fire and horses of fire. This order of God's angels almost exclusively uses chariots and horses. Though the passage apparently does not mention the appearance of an angelic rider, more than likely someone was needed to drive the chariot, and that someone was an angel. For this reason, this fourth order of God's angels was involved in the translation of Elijah.

The Ofannim are not employed as wheels of chariots. The wheels of chariots are inanimate objects.

In 2 King. 6:13–17, this angelic order was involved in a war against the Syrians and for the Jews. This proves that, though these angels' main function is either scouting or spying for the Lord God, they can fight in real wars and battles. Other angels do not have as their main function scouting or spying for the Lord God.

In Zechariah 1:7–15, God gave to Zechariah a very interesting vision. In this vision, Zechariah beheld with amazement a man riding upon a red horse and behind him were red, speckled, and white horses. Zechariah could not understand what he saw and sought aid in trying to understand it. The angel whom Zechariah saw riding upon a red horse explained that what he saw is those whom the Lord had sent to walk back and forth through the earth. This is the main function of this order of God's angels. These angels are the very invisible agencies of God who are sent forth as either scouts or spies to report on the conditions. (See vv. 8–11.) This is a clear proof that God is always interested in the ongoing affairs of the universe. The question that this brings up about God's omniscience will be undertaken at another time and another book.

In Zechariah 6:1–8, Zechariah's tenth vision was given. In this vision, Zechariah beholds four spiritual horse-chariots. These four spiritual horse-chariots had angelic riders upon them. It was the purpose of the riders of these spiritual chariots to go throughout the earth: the riders of the spiritual chariots with black horses to the north country, the riders of the spiritual chariots with white horses to go after them, the riders of the spiritual chariots with spotted horses to go forth toward the south country, and the riders of the spiritual chariots with bay horses to go throughout the earth. Their purpose in doing this was to find out the condition of the earth whether partially or completely. God used the riders of the spiritual chariots with the black and white horses to scout on the territory north of Israel. God used the riders of the spiritual chariots with the spotted horses to spy or scout on the territory south of Israel. The riders of the spiritual chariots with bay horses were ordered by God to spy or scout on all the territory of the earth.

The names of these angels found in Scripture are angel and man as witnessed by Zechariah 1:8–14. These angels rule over nothing. They are set apart from those who rule. They may be seen also as reserve fighters for God. Since they rule over nothing, the chief angels are ruled over directly by the Ofannim. So, the fourth order is bypassed, and the third order of angels is what rules directly over the fifth order.

These angels receive reports from the fifth order and receive and give out reports to all the other orders. Further, they give reports on the progress of the battles and wars being fought throughout the second heaven, the first heaven, or on the earth.

Besides this, these angels police other areas of the universe and especially the earth for God.

While all angels can ride spiritual horses and drive spiritual chariots, not all angels do this permanently. This order is the only one that does. This is the difference. While angels from the other orders occasionally ride upon spiritual horses and drive spiritual chariots, the angels found in this order do it permanently and continually throughout the universe as the very scouts and spies of the Most High God.

In reference to spiritual animals, there are countless other spiritual animals in heaven. (See Hebrews 11:6.) These other animals are not angels, but they have a spiritual nature. None of these other spiritual animals rebelled against God. The only spiritual animals that rebelled against God are those spiritual horses that fell along with their riders. Spiritual horses are not counted separately from their angelic riders. Though they are not angels, they are included as part of the angelic fourth order.

Chief Angels

These angels are the fifth most powerful. (See Deuteronomy 32:8; Daniel 10:1–21; 1 Thessalonians 4:16; Jude 9.) The chief angels are also called angelic princes, chief-rulers, and commander in chiefs.

Facts About the Chief Angels

The earliest mention of chief angels is found in Deuteronomy 32:8 from the Greek Septuagint. According to this text, God is seen to set the bounds of the nations according to the number of God's angels. This means that the number of nations equaled the number of angels that God has placed over the nations. These angels are chief angels, and only chief angels rule over nations. The book entitled, *The Testaments of the Twelve Patriarchs* also mentions this (8–10:10.) Besides this, Deuteronomy 32:8 proves that only godly angels resided over all the nations for a time. What happened? There were spiritual wars and battles found in the heavenlies. These battles caused some good angels to be defeated and have evil angels take their place. This kind of conflict over the nations is ongoing and has been continuing since God divided the nations. (See Genesis 10:32; 11:1–8.)

The chief angels are mentioned in Daniel 10:1–21. This passage mentions that Gabriel was detained by the satanic chief angel over the Medo-Persian Empire. It was only after Michael came that Gabriel could go to Daniel and give him the words about what would befall his people in the latter days. Gabriel said that when he left Daniel that he would return to fight with the satanic chief angel over the Medo-Persian Empire so that the satanic chief angel over the Greek Empire could come. This passage confirms that every kingdom and nation has angels over them. These angels are seen as the real power before them. Every kingdom and nation is measured by how powerful these angels are in spiritual conflicts. The very success of each kingdom and nation is determined by how powerful these angels are.

Gabriel, Michael, and the satanic angel over the Medo-Persian Empire are all chief angels: Gabriel and Michael being chief angels of God's kingdom and the satanic angel over the Medo-Persian Empire being the fallen chief angel of Satan's kingdom.

According to the Babylonian Talmud, the satanic chief angel of the Medo-Persian Empire was named Dubiel. This name means "bear-god." In Daniel 7:5, the Medo-Persian Empire appears as a bear, and the Jews concluded from this that the name of this satanic chief angel was the bear-god.[1] Rome is mentioned in the Babylonian Talmud as having a chief angel over it.[2]

In Daniel 12:1, Michael is seen as the godly chief angel over Israel. Therefore, since Israel has an angel over them, then other nations evidently have angels over them too.

According to 1 Thessalonians 4:16, the Lord God will descend from heaven by a word of command, by the voice of an archangel, and by the trumpet of God. Three things must occur simultaneously for the Rapture to occur.

The first thing is a word of command from Christ. This harmonizes with what was said by Christ about the resurrection of the dead in John 5:25. Christ said that the hour is coming when the dead will hear His voice of command and will arise and live in human incorruptible and immortal bodies.

The second thing is that an archangel will cry aloud that it is time for the Rapture.

The third thing is that the trumpet of God will sound. The trumpet is not a trumpet of an angel, but the trumpet of God the Word who is Christ. It is Christ Himself who will blow this trumpet to signal that the time has come for the Rapture. The archangel who will cry aloud will be Gabriel since he is the guardian angel of the Christian church. (See Daniel 8:16; 9:21; Luke 1:19–26.)

In Jude 9, it is recorded that Michael contended with Satan about the dead body of Moses. In Revelation 2–3, seven chief angels are seen to be over each church. In the New Testament, chief angels are called the Greek noun ἀρχάγγελος (ärkhängĕlōs) in 1 Thessalonians 4:16 and Jude 9. Instead of archangel, this Greek noun is better translated "chief angel."

Instead of having four groups of chief angels, there are only two groups:

+ The first group of chief angels is the most powerful chief angels and the fewest. They rule over the areas of the earth controlled by the kingdom of God. An example of this kind of angel is Michael who is the chief angel over Israel. (See Daniel 12:1.)

+ The second group of chief angels is less powerful than the first group of the chief angels and the most in number. They rule over planets controlled by the kingdom of God.

Why is the second group less powerful than the first group of chief angels? The reason for this can only be that God wanted the most powerful of the fifth order to rule over the areas of the earth controlled by the kingdom of God, because Satan tries with all vigor to take all the earth as his own. Proof of this is seen in the case of Michael since he is the guardian angel of Israel.

Common Angels

Common angels are the sixth most powerful order. These angels are the least powerful of all God's angels. More than 280 references to angels are made in Scripture. Out of these scriptures are found many references to the common angels. These angels are called common because they are the ones commonly used by God above all other orders while being the least powerful of all God's angels.

Facts About These Angels

In the Greek Septuagint and the New Testament, these angels are commonly known in the Greek as ἄγγελος (ängĕlōs). This means "angel." In the Masoretic Hebrew text, they are also known as the Hebrew noun מַלְאָךְ (mäläkh). This also means "angel."

These angels follow the orders of the chief angels, are ruled over by the chief angels, and are used in countless ways which humanity cannot fathom.

CHAPTER 5

Angelic Attributes Commonly Known

WHEN STUDYING THE nature of angels there can be great difficulties. The first is seen in defining what the term *person* means. Others are found in defining what *class, attributes, individuality,* or *nature* mean. These terms come from the understanding of Greek, Hebrew, and Latin languages.

- ◆ A person is a combination of both a complete nature and individuality. A person is that which by individuality possesses a separate copy of the same nature shared by a class of individuals or things.

- ◆ A class is a group of individuals or things that share the same nature.

- ◆ Attributes are those things that belong to and make up the nature.

- ◆ Individuality defines one's existence separately from any other. Individuality is the condition of existing as a separate person or thing from all others in a class with all in that class sharing the same nature. Then individuality makes certain changes, which define a difference between all others within a class or group.

These differences are not common to any other within a class or group. These differences may be attributes, things, actions, positions, or other such things.

◆ Nature is every attribute that every member of a class must necessarily share to belong to that same class. Therefore, nature is the kind of substance or stuff common to several individuals, persons, or things within a class.

Angels Are Spiritual Beings

In Psalm 104:4, the angels are said to be spiritual beings and are continuing to be by the sustaining power of God. The substance found in this verse is very powerful. The *present tense* is used instead of a *past tense*. What does this mean? It is a fact that this is the context found in Psalm 104:4. The rest of Psalm 104 denotes that the present tense must be used. The *present tense* does not mean that God is continuing to create angels repeatedly, but that it is God alone who causes angels to continue to be spiritual beings. God is the One who sustains their existence and the One alone who upholds them to continue to be spiritual beings. He is the cause and the source of their existence as spiritual beings. Without Him, the angels would not exist. (See Hebrews 1:1–3; James 1:17; Acts 17:24–25; 17:28.)

This very fact is what the Psalmist is saying. That unless God sustains and upholds all things that He has already created, it cannot last nor continue to exist. From Him comes the source of life, and without Him comes the source of death. On this account, God is the source of life while Satan is the source of death. Satan is the source of death in the sense that by his rebellion, death was created first as spiritual death. It was spiritual death and the power of Satan behind sin that invaded the world at the rebellion of humanity against God. (See Romans 5:12–14.)

The Greek verb ποιέω (pēěō) and the Hebrew verb עָשָׂה (äsäh) mean in this instance, "cause" or "make" in the sense that God is the One who continues to cause the angels to be spiritual beings. Such power is found in these verbs that the only way angels can continue to exist is by God sustaining and preserving them. Such power is found in these words that the thought also carries over into the conception that nothing can continue to exist without God's explicit stamp of approval upon it. God must allow it to continue and sustain it. (See Hebrews 1:1–3; James 1:17; Acts 17:24–25; 17:28.) If not, it cannot exist. This has great and powerful implications. Not even Satan and all his evil forces have the power to exist outside God's permission. The sovereignty of God is expressed here in this verse and it cannot be doubted. This verse also bears a witness to God's providence in His creation. His creation would fall to pieces if God did not involve Himself in its affairs.

The Greek noun πνεύμα (pnĕvmä) and the Hebrew noun רוּחַ (rūkhä) mean in this instance "spiritual being." Still, these nouns here do not have any reference to spiritual beings that are without bodily form. Undoubtedly, the expression *spiritual beings*, as it relates to the angels, denotes beings who were not created out of dust, but beings whom God created out of nonexisting matter of a nonexisting base. This matter is of a finer nature than what humans were created out of, a matter that far exceeds any elements of a lower standard, and a matter filled with the very glory of God.

The reference to His ministers as a "flaming fire," found in the last part of Psalm 104:4, reveals that the angels are quite old. The Jews believed that all of Psalm 104:4 has reference to angels, not only God continuing to cause them to be spiritual beings, but also causing them to continue to be a flaming fire.

The noun *angels* in Psalm 104:4 has reference to the class of spiritual beings mentioned here. The term "spiritual beings" has reference to the nature of angels. The term *ministers* has reference to the office of the angels. Angels are of the office of ministers since they minister to whomever God wants, whether it is He, His saints, or others. The angels may also be seen from this term as intercessors. The term *a flaming fire* has reference to the work of the angels since their work is in association with the Shekinah Presence.

Angels Invisible and/or Visible

Angels are beings who can transform themselves from being invisible to being visible and from being visible to invisible. Angels can transform themselves in this manner, according to their own will, but this transformation is under the direct supervision of the Lord God and is only carried out when the sovereignty of God orders it to occur. It is left up to God whether they remain invisible or become visible. This ability has been termed "Spirit Transformation." This transformation occurs at the place that they want to appear in the physical realm or disappear from that same realm.

Their invisibility is for the spiritual realm while their visibility is for the physical realm. Their invisibility is the only means by which they can exist in the spiritual realm. Their visibility is the only means by which they can exist in the physical realm. That angels can move from the physical realm to the spiritual realm, and from the spiritual realm to the physical realm at will, is well attested in Scripture. This is done by their ability to transform themselves from invisibility to visibility and back and forth as needed.

What is changed when angels appear visible? Their bodies, which consist of a spiritual substance, are changed into a physical substance. By this change, the substance, which was spiritual and could not be perceived by the five physical senses, can now be perceived by the physical senses. In other words, the structure of the angels is changed so that they can manifest themselves in the physical realm tangibly and visibly.

When angels appear visible, they are no longer in the spiritual realm. They have entered the physical realm for some purpose of God, or with a fallen angel for some purpose of Satan.

The spiritual realm is best defined as a "realm that the five physical senses—sight, hearing, touch, smell, and taste—cannot perceive." With the intervention of God, the soul of man can perceive the spiritual realm. The physical realm is best defined as a "realm that the five physical senses can perceive." Within this realm, which the five physical senses can perceive, spiritual beings also operate and by their spiritual senses are able to perceive it. Because of this ability, the spiritual senses can perceive both the spiritual realm and the physical realm. The five physical senses can only perceive the physical realm. This shows the superiority of the spiritual over the physical.

Demons and the human dead perceive the spiritual realm through spiritual properties from their spirits. By this they can imitate these spiritual senses. They really have not any kind of spiritual sense due to being disembodied. Demons and the human dead sense the physical realm in this manner. Both, being disembodied, are unable to exist in the physical realm.

The spiritual realm and physical realm can be called *worlds* instead of *realms.* The meaning is the same. The definitions of these realms promote the fact that each realm is just as real as the other. It must be known that the spiritual realm is mentioned throughout the Bible. It must always be remembered that to the writers of the Bible, the spiritual realm is as real as the physical realm. Indeed, they recognize that the spiritual realm is interwoven into the physical realm and the physical realm into the spiritual realm.

Comparing the tangible and material substances, which are found in the spiritual realm and in the physical realm reveals that those found in the spiritual realm will always be seen as intangible and immaterial according to the physical standards in which physical beings and things are identified. The reason is that the five physical senses cannot perceive them. However, the things found within the spiritual realm are just as tangible and visible to the things found in the physical realm. Consequently, the spiritual realm being tangible and visible does not mean that physical beings can perceive this by physical means. No! What is meant is that beings living in this realm can perceive it by spiritual means. On this account, a spiritual substance is tangible, and visible in the spiritual realm.

For example, how could Christ go to the underworld while His human body was in the tomb if the underworld were unreal, and intangible in the spiritual realm? (See Psalm 16:10; Luke 23:43; Ephesians 4:7–11.) Even further, how could Gabriel fight against the satanic chief angel of the Medo-Persian Empire as recorded in Daniel 10 unless each could see, touch, and hold each other in a fighting grasp? On the other hand, how could heaven be considered a better place if it did not have substance, or that substance was not tangible and material in its realm, the spiritual realm? (See Hebrews 11:16.)

Consequently, the bodily form of each angel is tangible and visible in the spiritual realm. The bodily form of each angel can be seen and touched by other spiritual beings. This does not mean that the bodily form of an angel cannot become material in the physical realm by the power of God. Their bodies can do that. The definition given of the spiritual realm does not deny the fact that in times, and even now, spiritual beings have appeared and can appear visibly in the physical realm. When this occurs, the spiritual beings are no more in the spiritual realm, but in the physical realm and can be perceived by the five physical senses.

This definition of the spiritual realm does not deny the fact spiritual beings can operate in the physical realm. Nor that demons can, through their power and possessions of humans and animals, affect the physical realm. By their power, they affect the physical realm while still existing in the spiritual realm. By their possession of humans and animals they are also able to affect the physical realm and manifest themselves in the physical realm though literally still existing in the spiritual realm. Since they are disembodied, they cannot abandon the spiritual realm and literally enter the physical realm. They can only manifest themselves in the physical realm through the possessed, which in turn pressures the subjects to manifest physically the presence of demons and those things that the demons are demanding to be manifested in the physical realm. In this indirect way, demons are able at least temporarily and partly to satisfy their physical lusts, wants, desires, and whatever else they can through another.

If demons cannot abandon the spiritual realm, then what about the times that they possess a person and enter the body of a victim? Both the spiritual realm and the physical realm are interwoven together and occupy the same space, but in different dimensions. Because of this, a demon can possess a person and still be in the spiritual realm. How? Both the victim and the demon occupy the same space though the victim is in the physical realm and the demon is in the spiritual realm. In this, the demon being disembodied can enter the body of a person, reside in the midst of the person, and still be in the spiritual realm and not in the physical realm. Angels are not disembodied; therefore, they cannot do this.

In Numbers 22:22–35, the angel of the Lord was first only seen by the ass in the vision. However, the body of an angel was not changed to become visible, but the power of God was impressed upon this animal's mind so that she could perceive the angel.

This passage confirms what many have thought—that animals can see angels in visions and talk with them. This fact is very interesting. It confirms that animals can see visions. In addition, it proves that animals can talk with angels. This is even more fascinating!

In Daniel 3:24–35, Genesis 18:2–33, 19:1–26, 32:24–30, and Judges 6:11–22, and 13:1–23, the angels mentioned are seen to be invisible first and then visibly appear. After their mission is completed they become invisible. Undeniably, the invisibility of the angels denotes that they are in the spiritual realm while the visibility of the angels denotes that they are in the physical realm.

Nevertheless, dealing with the spiritual realm as defined, it seems to create contradictions when we take into account the stories of Enoch and Elijah. These two men have never experienced physical death and yet live in heaven in their physical bodies. How does one reconcile this? Some have reconciled this by saying that flesh and blood cannot enter heaven. Therefore, stating that when Enoch and Elijah were translated, their bodies were resurrected and became similar to the human body of Christ. Nevertheless, if Enoch and Elijah were the first to receive these resurrected bodies, then the Scriptures are untrue. The Scriptures do not say that flesh and blood cannot enter heaven, but that flesh and blood cannot enter the kingdom of God. (See 1 Corinthians 15:50.) The glorified saints will inherit it. (See Romans 8:14–17; 1 Corinthians 4:20; 6:9–10; Galatians 5:21.) Why? All the saints will have resurrected bodies, which will be flesh and bone, not flesh and blood. Therefore, flesh and bone will inherit the kingdom of God, not flesh and blood. The resurrected bodies will have no blood. (See Luke 24:39.) In addition, since Christ is the first fruit of the permanent resurrection, and as such was the first who received a resurrected body, then how could Enoch and Elijah have one before Christ? (See John 20:17–20; 1 Corinthians 15:20–23; Hebrews 2:14–25.)

The early church clearly taught that in heaven Enoch and Elijah retained their natural bodies.[1] If this is true, then how did they stay in heaven? Heaven itself, or parts of it, can by God change from a spiritual nature to that of a physical nature. Therefore, Enoch and Elijah inhabit a special part of heaven, which became physical through divine power just for them.

Why do angels appear in visible form less now than they did in Old Testament times? There are several reasons:

- Many people are not praying or are not close enough to God for His angels to appear in this manner.

- Many people would become exalted in position if they saw an angel in this manner.

- Many would begin to worship the angels when they appeare in this manner, and institute angelic cults.

49

- Many people would not live by faith the way that they should if they saw an angel in this light.

- Fallen angels love to appear in this manner, as in the middle of the Tribulational Period. (See Revelation 12:7–9.)

- Since the appearance of God the Word in flesh, His death, and resurrection, God does not want to do anything that will take one's eyes off Christ. He alone is the way to God the Father (see John 14:6), and the only mediator between God and man (1 Timothy 2:5; Hebrews 8:6; 9:15; 12:24).

Colossians 1:16 proves quite well that angels have the power by God's will to change from being invisible to being visible and back and forth as needed.

Angels Work in the Physical Realm

The angels of God are not limited to just the spiritual realm. God created them so that they can feel just as home in the physical realm as they do in the spiritual realm though their primary realm of existence is the spiritual realm.

That angels can work in the spiritual realm is well attested by Scripture. (See Daniel 7–12; Psalm 103:20; 2 Kings 19:35; 2 Thessalonians 1:7; Job 1:6; 2:1; Zechariah 1–6.) As a result, God endowed angels with such a nature that would enable them to operate in the physical realm with no boundaries. Why would God create spiritual beings that could only operate in the spiritual realm when God needed beings that could operate in the physical realm to protect, watch over, maintain, and run it precept upon precept? In other words, the works of angels are done to aid God in His providential working in the affairs of His creation. On this account, angels are seen as agents of God's providence concerning both the physical and the spiritual and both the body and soul of man. To achieve this, God in both the spiritual realm and the physical realm dispatches angels. (See Matthew 18:10; Revelation 5:11; Psalm 90:10–12; 2 Kings 19:35.)

Angels can work in the physical realm in two ways: (1) Angels working in the physical realm while still staying in the spiritual realm, as with Balaam, (see Numbers 22:22–35); (2) The appearance of the angels in the physical realm in a visible and physical body as in the cases of Abraham and Lot. (See Genesis 18–19.) In the first manner, the angels operate in the physical realm, not personally, but from the spiritual realm through their actions to manipulate the situations found in the physical realm. In the second manner, the angels operate in the physical realm, personally being in it and not in the spiritual realm.

The working of God's angels in the physical realm is seen clearly in the scriptures given. Studying very carefully the work of God's angels in the physical realm, angels can apparently work in every aspect of the physical realm and have control over the physical order of things found inside. Angels can, always in accordance to the will of God, interfere with the laws of nature in the physical realm for the greater good and for the cause of God the Almighty. As such, angels transcend the laws of nature.

The very appearance of the angels in the physical realm shows that they have the ability to override the laws of nature in the physical realm at will. They can change them or lay them aside, always in accordance to the providence of God, to fulfill the will of God in the physical realm. However, their interference with the laws of nature is only temporary.

If the angels would disable the laws of nature permanently, then the whole physical realm would be in chaos. Such chaos in the physical realm would result in its utter destruction. No planet, star, galaxy, human, or animal could exist. There is such importance in an angel interfering with the laws of nature that God has limited how long this can occur. Therefore, the disabling of the laws of nature by angels has a time limit and is only local, not universal. For example, an angel who overrides the laws of nature, in accordance to God's will, in a town for a mission of the Lord God only affects the laws of nature in that town, not throughout the physical realm. Nevertheless, the disabling of the laws of nature by angels can also be seen to occur over a whole nation or a whole continent in the earth and in the heavenlies over certain sections. However, when it comes to the whole physical realm, God only does this if it is needed.

Any kind of miracle done by an angel through the power of God is an act of overriding the laws of nature. So a miracle is a supernatural act of God that overrides the laws of nature that have been in place since the rebellion of Lucifer and Adam. Notice that the laws were introduced as a result of Lucifer's rebellion and then suspended due to the restoration of creation. When Adam sinned, they were again active and have been ever since. Another definition is that a miracle is a supernatural act of God that is entirely outside the control of the laws of nature and is not limited by physical laws.

For example, one law of nature is the law of physical death, in effect since the rebellion of Lucifer and Adam. When God Himself resurrects a human from physical death, the law of physical death is disabled so that the resurrection can come about. This situation is seen with Lazarus when he died. The law of physical death was overridden so that Lazarus would arise from the dead. (See John 11:1–43.) However, because this resurrection was not the permanent one, which Christ is the firstfruit of, Lazarus faced mortal death again and the law of death came upon him again. (See 1 Corinthians 15:20.)

Another example is found when Christ ascended. (See Acts 1:9.) Christ, having a body of flesh and bone—without blood, since His blood physically was poured out at the cross for humanity's sins—was lifted up from the earth. Something similar to this is seen with Philip, when he was transported from the eunuch at the water, to Azotus still having a body of flesh, bone, and blood. (See Acts 8:39–40.) While Christ after His resurrection obtained a human body glorified, resurrected, and immortal, it still is a body of flesh and bone.

Another example is found in Acts 12:7. Here, the law of solid matter was disabled. The angels can bypass inanimate physical obstacles—that is, go through solid doors, windows, prison bars, and solid walls—without trouble. Inanimate physical obstacles cannot hinder spiritual substance.

Only God transcends the universe. What does this mean? God is the only One who can work outside the universe or can work inside the universe everywhere simultaneously whether through His omnipresence or through other means, such as His angels. Angels and all other beings cannot do this.

Angels Have Limited Knowledge

Though Matthew 24:36 and Mark 13:32 show very explicitly that angels are limited in knowledge, their limit of knowledge far exceeds the knowledge that humanity has. Such knowledge that man has is only considered as a drop of water when comparing the knowledge that the angels possess. Secrets and mysteries that humanity could never imagine are already known by the angels and are part of their knowledge. Such counsel has God given the angels that their knowledge far exceeds any other created class of beings. Their knowledge is such that beholding it is marvelous. But their knowledge is considered as nothing when compared with the knowledge of God.

Angels are greater than men in knowledge, although they are not omniscient. God intended them to have great knowledge, but finite knowledge. Their knowledge involves commonly the secrets of the spiritual realm and the physical realm. The angels know such secrets that are beyond a human's capacity to grasp them.

The fact that angels are ignorant of certain things is well noted in 4 Ezra 4:51–52, where an angel was unable to answer a question put to him. Angels are seen to be ignorant of the exact time of the Second Coming, but there is more about which they are ignorant. They do not understand the mystery of the Gospel in its fullness or the Church in its fullness. It is this reason the Church is teaching them wisdom. They want to understand more deeply the mystery that so encompasses the Church in their eyes. As such, the angels are limited, and even know their limitations.

The key Greek word in Matthew 24:36 and Mark 13:32 is the Greek verb οἶδα (ēthä). This Greek verb proves that the angels do not know the exact time of the Second Coming. Why? The exact time of the Second Coming of Christ is not a concern for them. Their office as minister does not conclude that they must know this. The fact that angels do not know this shows their finiteness and proves that they are not God, but only created beings.

The angels of God despise all the knowledge of the world and short-lived things, which Satan and his allies glory over possessing. This does not mean that the angels of God are ignorant of this knowledge, but they want to put all their being in holiness and the things that pertain to holiness. Why? Because God is holy above all things, and they long to continue to be close to Him.

Angels Are Intelligent and Wise

Through the thin line of 2 Samuel 14:17, men on the earth are seen to have greatly esteemed angels for their vast intelligence. This intelligence far exceeds mankind's intelligence to discern good from evil, but the angels' intelligence is no match for the intelligence that God has had for all eternity.

What does the angels' intelligence consist of? The entire intelligence that they have can be summed up with in one statement: the angels are intelligent of everything that God so wills, and wants them to know and understand to establish and cause His will and purpose.

Studying 2 Samuel 14:17 in the Greek Septuagint and the Masoretic Hebrew text, the best meaning of the infinitives is "to hear the good and the evil." This is interesting. Angels of God are revealed by the meaning of these infinitives as ones who listen to the conversations of the good and of the evil. According to this, one key way that the angels discern who is of the saints and who is of the wicked is by what they hear a person to speak. Just by what a person speaks, the angels of God discern who belongs to either the saints or the wicked. If a person is a saint, then his conversations will change to that which is holy. However, if a person is wicked, then his conversations will be anything but holy. Therefore, one key in which angels can discern the evil from the good is by a person's conversations.

No wonder Solomon warned the saints, and all others, about implications of the tongue in Proverbs 18:21. Such power is in the tongue, and what is said that it has the power of life and death. How? The use of a tongue correctly and in holiness will cause a person to receive blessings from God. On the contrary, the use of a tongue incorrectly and in wickedness will cause a person to receive curses from God. God and the angels are watching and listening to what people say. Because of this, it is in the person's ability and will to receive either the curses or the blessings of God by controlling his tongue. Man's tongue is the manifestation of what he has in his heart and his will about obedience to God.

Additionally, the angels are seen to be intelligent beings from their functions of praising, rejoicing, worshiping, teaching, and ministering to the prophets and the saints. Only intelligent beings could accomplish the many diverse functions the angels accomplish. No other kind of being could achieve this.

Studying 2 Samuel 14:20, angels are seen as wise. God Himself, being wise and intelligent, would not create beings that were only intelligent without wisdom. That would be illogical. Angels have such wisdom that the wisdom of Solomon, with all its majesty, could not stand up against it. In fact, the only wisdom that far exceeds their wisdom is the wisdom of God. The Creator has infinite wisdom, while the wisdom of the angels is finite in form.

The wisdom that angels possess is godly in form. While their wisdom is godly in form, it still looks into the affairs of the ungodly, knowing that way will lead to damnation. They also remember Satan's rebellion against God and recollect the judgments brought against the rebels that participated in it. But with all the wisdom that the angels of God do have, they have not become exalted. Why? Because their wisdom is finite, and they know of this each day by their growing in wisdom, for the church is teaching them wisdom.

According to some, the intelligence of angels is so great that they know all things that are occurring on the earth. Yet, 2 Samuel 14:20 does not say that. According to the Greek Septuagint, the things that God's angels know are not all the things that are occurring on the earth, but a considerable amount. The Greek adjective πᾶς (päs) not having the article before it can only mean that the angels of God do not know all things, but only many things. This shows that the angels are limited in knowledge and intelligence, and are finite.

Angels Are Patient and Humble

To begin with this topic of discussion, it is very important to cite what is said about patience in the work entitled *Pastor of Hermas:*

> You see, then, that patience is sweeter than honey, and useful to God, and the Lord dwells in it.[2]

Therefore, in the work *Pastor of Hermas,* patience is seen as sweeter than honey and even the Lord dwells in it. Beyond this document's insight into patience, it is seen from Tertullian, an Early Church Father, in his work on patience what he says about this subject:

> Accordingly, it is patience which is both subsequent and antecedent to faith. In short, Abraham believed God, and was accredited by him with righteousness; but it was patience which proved his faith, when he was bidden to immolate his son, with a view to (I would not say the temptation, but) the typical attestation of his faith…Deservedly then was he "blessed," because he was "faithful," deservedly "faith-ful," because "patient."[3]

Such importance is patience that Tertullian prescribes it to be both subsequent and antecedent to faith. Such importance is patience in the life of Abraham that it proved that he had faith in God.

Tertullian, using the example of Abraham, shows that the early church understood that a holy life will have patience in it. Nevertheless, if a person has faith in God, then one heavenly attribute found in that person will be patience. So, patience proves faith. While patience proves faith in God, impatience disproves faith in God. This is the state of Satan and all his rebellious hosts. This is the state of all wicked men and women. On this account, since patience is from God, it would not be all surprising that God's angels have patience too. Impatience is the creation of Satan.

To show an example of God's angels having patience look at Numbers 22:22–35. The angel of the Lord appears not to bless Balaam, but to stop him any way that was possible. This means even by death, if it became necessary. This was because Balaam was going to curse God's beloved Israel.

According to the lust of Balaam over great wealth, he went on his way riding on an ass and with two of his servants. While everything seemed all right, nothing was. The angel of the Lord met them with his sword drawn. However, none of the men saw him. Only the ass beheld this angel. The ass was afraid that she would not go the way that Balaam wanted him to go, but into a field. When the ass turned aside and went into a field, Balaam was so angry that he hit her.

The very fact that the ass went the other way still does not remove the possibility that the angel could have killed him on the spot if the ass had not turned and went into the field.

Instead of the angel killing Balaam this time, the angel patiently went even farther and stood in the avenues of vineyards with a fence being on one side and another on the other side. This time the ass seeing the angel of the Lord crushed Balaam's foot against the wall, and he hit her again. This time Balaam became even angrier. Yet even during this time, the angel was still showing a great portion of patience. Why? The angel could have killed him this time, but he did not. The third time was the last. Here, the angel of God went farther and came and stood in a narrow place where turning to the right or to the left was impossible. When the ass saw the angel this time, she laid down on the ground with Balaam on her back. When this occurred, Balaam was extremely angry and struck the ass with his staff. At this time, God opened the mouth of the ass and she spoke to Balaam after which God opened the eyes of Balaam so he could see the angel of the Lord standing before him.

Three times, the angel could have killed Balaam, but the angel showing a heavenly patience was very patient and did not act hastily. As this story shows, angels are not only patient, but humble. This truth is seen in that the angels did not bring forth a blasphemous condemnation against certain ones mentioned in 2 Peter 2:11. Notice that angels do not want any glory whatever for themselves, but they want all the glory and honor to go to God whom they serve.

Whom does "them" refer to in 2 Peter 2:11? The Greek phrase κατ' αὐτῶν (kät ävtōn) in 2 Peter 2:11 is connected to δόξας. This means "glories" in 2 Peter 2:10. The Greek noun δόξα (thōxä) has reference to fallen angels mentioned in 2 Peter 2: 4–5. The fallen angels mentioned in 2 Peter 2:4–5 are those who invaded the physical realm, left the spiritual realm for a considerable time, caused their bodies to become physical, and cohabited with women to corrupt the bloodline so that Messiah could not come and destroy the works of Satan. (See 1 John 3:8; Genesis 6:1–4; 6:4–7; 6:11–13; Jude 6–7; 2 Peter 2:4–5; 2:10–11.) If Satan had succeeded in the complete corruption of humanity through these fallen angels, then no undefiled genetic line would have been found through which Christ could be born. If Satan had succeeded in this endeavor then God coming as man would have been impossible. They are the fallen angels against whom the good angels do not bring forth a blasphemous condemnation, because of the diabolical act that they did after the original rebellion instigated by Satan. (See Ezekiel 28:12–19; Isaiah 14:12–15; Matthew 13:9; 13:39; John 13:2; Revelation 12:1–17.) That the Sons of God in Genesis 6:1–4 were in fact fallen angels had never been disputed, but maintained by the Jewish Synagogue, by Hellenistic Jews at and before the time of Christ, and by the Christian church until the fourth century.

It should be recognized that this diabolical act happened before Noah's flood and after the flood. In the middle of the Tribulational Period, this diabolical act will happen again. When? In the middle of the Tribulational Period, all fallen angels loosed will be thrown out of the heavenlies and invade the earth. (See Revelation 12:7–10.) In this invasion, the fallen angels will appear tangible, being in the physical realm. At this time, the beauty of these spiritual beings will carry many women both married and unmarried away and cause them to commit fornication with them. The result will be as it was in Genesis 6:1–4. Monsters of gigantic size—half-breeds, angelic hybrids, the giants—will be the offspring of this union just like it was before Noah's flood and afterward too for some time. Christ also spoke of this when He said that as in the days of Noah so will it be before His Second Coming. (See Matthew 24:37–38; Luke 17:26–27.) An invasion of fallen angels occurred in the days of Noah. (See Genesis 6:1–4.) In 2 Peter 2:10 and Jude 8, the Greek noun δόξα is used for fallen angels. In these same passages, the fallen angels are the same.

The idea is that if good angels are so humble that they do not bring forth a blasphemous condemnation against the fallen angels who invaded the physical realm and cohabited with women, what rights do false teachers and deceivers of God's Word have to degrade these same fallen angels? Though these angels are fallen, the majesty of these same angels is still found in them. The majesty is the very imprint of God. Therefore, when anyone brings forth a blasphemous condemnation against even this group of fallen angels already bound, that person is touching God, for that person is saying how God could create something such as this. He is degrading the sovereignty of God and His permissive will. (See Acts 13:18; 14:16; 16:7; 1 Corinthians 10:13; Genesis 20:6; Luke 22:31; Genesis 2:15–3:21; Romans 9:22–23; Psalm 105:14; 1 Samuel 8:5–22; Mark 1:34; Luke 8:32, 51; Mark 5:19; 5:37.) The word *suffer* in said scriptures means "to allow or permit."

The good angels remember what these fallen angels were before their rebellion with Satan and their attempt to pollute the bloodline. So, they speak solemnly and sorrowfully, not in a coarse violent language. On this account, the false teachers were evidently so profane and blasphemous that they scoffed at these fallen angels, making fun of them, judging them, and condemning them over what they had done thinking themselves better than these angels.

In Scripture, 2 Peter 2:11–12 reveals to the saints to avoid irreverence to even these fallen angels, due to God. Though these angels are fallen and did that diabolical deed of unspeakable things, they are God's angels in the sense of receiving from Him their origin, though not in a fallen state. This fact is assuredly a great mark of humility. Though the good angels are greater than these fallen angels in power, they lower themselves in importance to show that it is not their place to condemn these fallen angels confined in Tartarus. (See 2 Peter 2:4.)

Angels Are Joyful

Can anyone conceive the joy that comes from angels? No, for in order to conceive that great joy totally, a person would have to be an angel of God. The reason the angels of God have joy can be seen in that they are not rebels against God, nor thrown away from His presence. (See Luke 15:7–10.) God did not count them evil and rebels just because other angels rebelled with Satan. No! God confirmed them and declared that they are without sin. On this account, the angels of God have a lot to be joyful about. Neither did they follow Satan nor will they receive the condemnation and punishment awaiting Satan and his followers.

Why are they joyful over a sinner being saved? For everytime a sinner is saved:

- ◆ It confirms the eternal plan of God.

- ◆ It confirms that they made the right choice.

- ◆ It confirms that Christ has conquered Satan and all his followers through the power of the blood.

- ◆ It confirms that in Christ there is victory.

- ◆ It confirms that they are holy and sinless.

- ◆ It confirms that they are redeemed from the implications of the fall of humanity.

- ◆ It confirms that they have escaped the damnation that will come upon all the wicked beings in the Lake of Fire.

Angels Are Powerful and Mighty

The power and might that the angels have is inconceivable at this time for humans. This power and might are established by God's Word (see Psalm 33:6–9; John 1:1–3; Colossians 1:16), by God's will, and by God's sovereignty. (See Hebrews 1:3; 14; Acts 17:24–25; James 1:17.)

According to Psalm 103:20 from the Greek Septuagint, the might of angels is based upon their power. In other words, the foundation of the angels' might is their power. So, the might of the angels is a visible manifestation of their power.

The Greek noun δύναμις (thēnämēs) refers to the outward manifestations of God's power. The Greek noun ἰσχύς (ēskhēs) has reference to the intrinsic power that God gave each of them. Consequently, the Greek noun δύναμις concerns the visible and tangible manifestation of the supernatural power that the angels possess, which is expressed here by the Greek noun ἰσχύς. The manifestation of this supernatural power is like many upon many tons of dynamite exploding at once and in one place. The power itself is indescribable and inconceivable to mere men. (See 2 Kings 19:35; Psalm 103:20; Revelation 18:1–21.) As such, angels are stronger than man can imagine.

In Revelation 10:1 and 18:21, the Greek adjective ἰσχυρός (ēskhērōs) is used to denote that the angels who appeared before John were inherently strong. The strength spoken of is not an outward manifestation of this power, but strong by the very nature of being. The Greek adjective ἰσχυρός shows that in these and all angels is found absolute angelic power. This Greek adjective denotes also the power itself that the angels possess instead of the manifestation of that power.

Since God is the true source of the angels' power, then they are dependent upon Him for it being sustained. God has both permitted and commanded its use. Consequently, their power is restricted. They are unable to do things that are contrary to the will of God.

Angels Are Completely Good

In 1 Samuel 29:9, angels are referred to as good. According to 1 Chronicles 16:34, Psalm 25:8, 34:8, 86:5, 118:29, 136:1, and 145:7, 9, God is completely good. In 2 Maccabees, 11:6 calls angels good. Both God and angels are referred to as good although Matthew 19:17, Mark 10:18, and Luke 18:19 state that only God is good. How do we account for this contradiction? Simply, God is the source of all goodness. Therefore, any goodness found in God's created beings comes from God. Consequently, the goodness found in His angels is seen to be completely good since its source is God.

The goodness of God flows through the good angels. This goodness is inherent. What does this mean? That God gave to the angels this goodness at their creation. It flows from Him, and therefore He is the source. This goodness made and makes their whole nature inherently good. The fallen angels rejected this goodness and accepted perverseness and evil. So, the fallen angels became inherently evil.

The same thing occurred at man's creation. God gave to man this goodness at his creation. It flows from God as the source. This made humanity become inherently good. However, all humanity at their rebellion against their Creator rejected this goodness and accepted perverseness and evil, instead. (See Genesis 2:15–3:21; Romans 3:9–10,22–23; Psalm 14; Isaiah 53:6; Romans 3:19; 5:12; 1 John 3:8–10; John 8:44; Romans 7; Ephesians 4:18; Jeremiah 17:9–10; Job 14:4; 15:14; 25:4–6; Psalm 2:5; 58:3; Genesis 6:5–12; Deuteronomy 32:5; Psalm 14:1–3; Proverbs 20:6–9; Jeremiah 16:12; Galatians 3:22.) Then, humanity became inherently evil. It is only by accepting Christ and His redemptive work that anyone can become inherently good in the sense that it is nothing he does that makes him good, but it is everything that God does through His goodness. (See Isaiah 64:6; Psalm 30:4; 47:8; 60:6; 97:12; 108:7; Jeremiah 23:9; Amos 4:2; Hebrews 12:10.)

In Matthew 19:17, Mark 10:18, and Luke 18:19, Christ makes a very important statement, after a man says that He is good. Christ proves that only God is good. In addition, He proves that any goodness found in anyone else is not because of the person himself, but because of the goodness of God flowing through him. For this reason, God is the source of all goodness. Even when a sinner does well, it is because of God's influence upon that sinner's life that interferes with the influence of Satan. There is a struggle between God's influence and Satan's influence over that sinner's life. As long as that person is unsaved, the controlling influence over his life is Satan's with only God's influence interfering on occasions. The opposite is so true when a person is saved. The controlling influence over a person's life is God's with Satan's influence trying to interfere with the relationship. (See Romans 6:6; 7:14–25; 8:6–16; Galatians 5:16–18; Colossians 3:5–10; 2 Corinthians 5:17; Acts 26:18; Ephesians 4:24; 2 Peter 2:19.)

In Matthew 19:17, Mark 10:18, and Luke 18:19 Christ declares that He is God. Christ says since there is no one good except God and since Christ is good, then Christ is God. The question that Christ asked was to let the man know that He is God. The man himself perceived Christ's deity.

That Christ is holy, good, and sinless is well attested in Scripture. (See Acts 3:14; 2 Corinthians 5:21; Hebrews 4:15; 7:26; 1 Peter 2:22; 1 John 3:5; Isaiah 53:11; Psalm 45:7; John 6:38; 8:29, 46; Galatians 4:4–5; 2 Corinthians 5:21; 1 Peter 2:21.)

Note that Christ did not tell the man "Follow God," but "Follow Me." This is a very strong testimony of Christ's deity.

Angels Are Holy and Have Glory

In Job 5:1 from the Greek Septuagint, Daniel 4:37c from the Greek Septuagint, Luke 9:26, Mark 8:38, Revelation 14:10, and Matthew 25:31, angels are said to be ἅγιος (äyēōs). This word, which is a Greek adjective, means "holy." The same Greek adjective is also often used of God in the Greek Septuagint and in the New Testament.

What is meant by the word *holy* concerning the angels of God? The angels of God are in a position of holiness and in a state of holiness. The position of holiness is understood to mean that the angels of God in God's sight are holy. The state of holiness is understood to mean that the angels of God exist in holiness without any hint of sin or moral impurity. Accordingly, angels are without sin and are not able to sin. (See Mark 8:28; Revelation 18:1.) So, the position of holiness is how God sees them. The state is how they are existing. Hence, God not only sees them as holy, but they exist as holy. Therefore, the angels of God exist in absolute purity without spot or blemish.

While the angels of God are existing in holiness, the source of this holiness cannot be the angels themselves, but God. (See Revelation 15:4.) On this account, the holiness found in the angels has as a source God Himself. The divine attribute of God such as God's holiness flows from the Lord God into the angels' nature, which causes them to imitate the divine character of God. While the attribute holiness is inherent to the angels of God, its source is God, and it is God who brought forth that attribute in the angels' nature. He continues to sustain that attribute in good angels because He is holy.

In Revelation 18:1, angels are said to have glory. This is their personal glory. It comes from God. Their glory flows from Him to them. For this account, the glory is inherent to their nature, but its source is God alone.

Angels Are Inferior to God

Studying Psalm 8:4–5, and Hebrews 1:7–8, angels are seen as inferior to God. It is God alone who sustains their existence. It is God alone who created them, and it is God alone who upholds their existence and continues to allow them to exist.

In Hebrews 1:7–8, three words are used to describe the inferiority of angels toward God: the first word is *maketh*, the second is *angels*, and the third is *ministers*. The word *maketh* uncovers the fact that God alone is sustaining their existence, and revealing the angels' inferiority to God. The second word, *angels*, shows that the angels were created by God. The third word, *ministers*, reveals the inferiority of the angels to God in that the angels are God's ministers ready to be employed as He wants.

There are many passages that display the inferiority of the angels to God their Creator. (See Colossians 1:16; Matthew 6:10; 26:53; 1 Kings 8:27; John 1:1–3; Job 1:6; 2:1; Psalm 96:7; Hebrews 1:6; Deuteronomy 32:43; Revelation 4–5.) They are established by God's Word, by God's will, and by God's sovereignty. (See Psalm 33:6–9; John 1:1–3; Colossians 1:16; Hebrews 1:3; 1:14; Acts 17:24–25; James 1:17.)

Angels Are Completely Obedient to God

Since God is holy and demands absolute obedience to His will, then it is very well acknowledged by God's nature that the angels would also be completely obedient to Him. God demands absolute obedience to His will. Anything less than this, God will not accept. Therefore, if any moral code or law is sinned against and not repented of that one unrepented sin will damn the soul. So holy is God that He demands His created beings to be holy. Therefore, so holy is God that He demands obedience more than sacrifice.

According to Psalm 103:20, so anxious are the angels to obey God that even before He speaks and commands them what they will do, they are in a state of readiness. The angels are not only in a state of holiness, but also a state of readiness. They are ready to obey the Lord God who confirmed them, declaring that they are holy and did not throw them out with the angels who fell. So much have the angels to be thankful for that they are eternally ready to obey the voice of God as He beckons them.

The entire nature of the angels is set to obey God. This was what was so disastrous to the fallen angels. For when they disobeyed God they were turning their backs completely upon the purpose for which they were created. Their rebellion was such a shock to their nature that they have never recovered from what they did to themselves. It was like pulling out of their nature their purpose for existing. Their lives are seen as a wilderness without any life-giving water. Such are their lives, that thousands upon thousands times a day do they long for the cooling life-giving water that can only be found in being in fellowship with the Lord God. Such miseries are found in the lives of the fallen angels and all spiritual rebels of God that they seek to gather all that they can to share in their misery. The dictum is so true: "Misery loves company."

In Matthew 26:53, Christ in His voluntary subordinate state and as the saints' perfect example, declared that if He wanted to He could ask God the Father to send Him more than twelve legions of angels to help Him. (See John 13:15; 1 Peter 2:21; 1 John 2:6; Matthew 11:29; Philippians 2:5.) This indicates that the instant an order is given by God for the angels to do something they immediately begin to do it. This is the state of readiness that the angels are in. This should be an example of just how ready the saints need to be to obey God and do His will.

Further, it must be mentioned that angels carry out God's will for those whom God favors to be helped and aided. (See Luke 1:28, 30; Numbers 20:16; Acts 5:19–20; Daniel 3:28; 7–9.)

Angels Are Created Beings Made by Christ

According to Colossians 1:16, the angels are a class of spiritual beings who have been completely created in a single simultaneous act of creation. Accordingly, no new creations of angels have or will occur. The creating act is over. God has all the angels that He needs, even with the fall of Satan and his forces. This verse proves that Christ created the angels. In essence, He is the reason all created things were created. Angels are a direct creation of God that occurred or took place simultaneously. Before their creation, they did not exist.

The anarthrous construction–or, without the article—of both the Greek and Hebrew nouns in Genesis 1:1 demands that creation itself was instantaneous, yet in order. While all things were created instantaneously, there was an order. On this account, from Job 38:6–7, an order of creation connected to Genesis 1:1 and Nehemiah 9:6 is seen. First came God's heaven also known as the third heaven (2 Corinthians 12:2; Genesis 1:1); second, came the angels (Job 38:4–7; Ezekiel 28:15; Colossians 1:16–18); third, came the second heaven (Genesis 1:1; Psalm 8:3; 19:1; 147:1; Isaiah 40:26; Colossians 1:16); fourth, came the earth, its heaven, and its inhabitants (Genesis 1:1; Isaiah 45:18; Hebrews 11:3.)

According to Job 38:6–7, the angels were already created when God originally created the earth, its heaven, and its inhabitants. Yet, this was done not in time, but in order of an instantaneous creation. In Genesis 1:1, the noun of time being used in the anarthrous construction emphasizes very strongly that creation itself was brought forth not in time, but separately from time and in order. Creation could not have been created in a fixed number of days, months, or years, but separately from time. Since the noun of time found in Genesis 1:1 demands that creation itself existed before time, then God created creation instantaneously.

A division of the early church held onto an instantaneous creation. Men like Basil, Gregory of Nyssa, and Augustine taught that there was an instantaneous creation before the six days. In essence, these three and other men taught that there are mentioned two separate creations in Genesis 1:1–2:25. The first was instantaneous, done outside time. (See Genesis 1:1.) The second creation was literally a restoration. (See Genesis 1:3–31; 2:4–14.)[4]

In dealing with many scriptures, the church fathers took various opinions It is apparent that they taught one passage of scripture at one time one way and at another time another way. Their audience or focus caused them to change their perspective on a given scripture. Further, it is not surprising that some of the same church fathers are noted as following more than one view on Creation. For their audience and for that time, the church fathers were following a definite opinion, and that must be our focus. While the tenet that God created the universe was and is an essential doctrine of Christianity, the means or how Creation occured was freely interpreted more than one way by the church fathers and on occasion by the same church father.

Scientists advocate that space and time began simultaneously. This is expected. In the manner that God created the universe, it seems that this is true. Yet creation itself existed before time according to Genesis 1:1. All creation does not transcend time, but must exist in it to be active. Then at the point of creation, there was a suspension of these activities, and these activities were never begun until time itself began. It is like God created the universe, and, until time itself was created, all that creation was frozen in suspension still existing, but not being able to be active. This suspension may be something similar to suspended animation. The universe until time itself was created was seen as being in a state of inactivity, not moving or acting. It took the creation of time to set in motion the universe so that it is active and truly shows that it exists.

The fact that the angels were praising the Lord as He created the earth proves that while all things were created instantaneously, there is found order in that creation. Basically, the angels were created instantaneously with praises of the Lord in their mouth. The first thing spoken by the angels was praises to the One who made them.

The fact that God created the angels after He created His heaven, as concerning order not in time, is only logical since God first created the places where inhabitants would reside and then the inhabitants.

According to Jude 6–7, the habitation of the angels is the spiritual realm. Then, the angels were created after the creation of the spiritual realm not in time, but in order. God's heaven is part of the spiritual realm. Therefore, the creation of the spiritual realm is in the same order that God's heaven, even His abode, was created. The underworld itself was added to the spiritual realm after the rebellion of Satan and his followers according to Matthew 25:41.

The second heaven is part of the physical realm. As a result, the creation of the physical realm occurred in the same order that the second heaven was created. Other things were added to the physical realm after this in order, not in time. The earth and its heaven were added afterward.

The size of the spiritual realm and the physical realm are the same since both realms are interwoven together. The size of the universe is the same size of both the spiritual realm and the physical realm. The term *universe* is best defined as "a sphere that encompasses into itself both the physical realm and the spiritual realm." The universe continues to expand. This undeniable truth is based upon God's sovereignty, providence, and, especially, His transcendence. Since God can work outside the universe, then something outside the universe must exist. This something will be used by God to allow the universe to continue to expand. This something is non-universal space or space that is not found in the universe. It is this that the universe continues to expand in. When the universe comes in connection with it, it becomes space as found in the universe and such part of the universe. This non-universal space came into being before the universe. God even created this in Genesis 1:1, though it is not considered part of creation as emphasized by the Bible, nor is it part of the saints' inheritance. Therefore, space is divided into two kinds: the first is non-universal space, or the space that is not part of the universe while the second is universal space or the space that is part of the universe.

Before these two types of space, there is found God who lived in spacelessness and timelessness. God is "from everlasting to everlasting." (See Psalm 41:13; 90:2; 100:5; 103:17; 106:48.)

The purpose of the angels' creation was to have fellowship with God, to be obedient to God, to glorify God, and to serve Him willingly in complete purity and perfection.

The Greek phrase τά πάντα (tä pända) found in Colossians 1:16 establishes that Christ created everything. This Greek phrase signifies that Christ created the entirety of creation. This Greek phrase was found in Revelation 4:10 and denotes the same thing.

In Nehemiah 9:6, Ezra in a prayer declares from the Greek Septuagint "....and you are causing all things to live." God is the source of all things that were created. This means the angels, as well. Since God is the source of the angels' existence, then He created them too. The same Greek phrase seen in Colossians is also seen in Nehemiah 9:6. Here it shows that God is the Creator of everything created and that He sustains all these things in their existence. The Greek phrase τὰ πάντα found in Nehemiah 9:6 arrives at the conclusion that everything created was created by God in the heavenlies, on the earth, and in the seas, and it is He who sustains it. This Greek phrase also has reference to creation in its state of perfection and sinlessness. According to Ecclesiastes 3:11, God created all things perfect and sinless. When the Greek adjective πᾶς (päs) is without the article in Nehemiah 9:6, it describes the creation being torn to pieces after the rebellion of Satan. Creation was torn to pieces when Satan and all his allies rebelled. Since then it cannot be seen as perfect and sinless. Why? For creation to be perfect and sinless the eradication and removal of Satan, all his forces, and all rebellious humans from God's creation must be carried out with their utter destiny being the Lake of Fire. Unequivocally, God is not responsible for their state and does not claim that He created them in that shape and manner. Ezra so honored God that he believed that God is not responsible for the evil beings and things in the heavenlies, on the earth, and in the seas, and did not create them in that shape and manner. Though God created everything, Ezra makes it known to all skeptics that God did not create sin, evil, and the state of evil. The consequences of evil and evil itself spring from the rebels' own free will.

Angels Praise and Worship the Divine Trinity

The angels recognize that God so demands worship that they are in a state of readiness. They are ready, not only to obey God, but to worship Him anytime. Therefore, one attribute of the angels is that they can worship God.

The Greek verb προσκυνέω (prōskēněō) is used in Hebrews 1:6 and Revelation 4:10. As it relates to the holy act of worship by the angels, it denotes to do reverence, homage, and worship to the divine persons truthfully, honestly, and completely without any pretense. As seen, the worship of God by the angels is something beyond human perception and actions.

Human worship of God cannot be as genuine as the worship given by the holy angels of God. Such purity of worship without any pretense is seen in the angels' act of worship toward God that it is sickening to try to compare human worship of the Holy God to theirs. Such splendor and excellence are found in the angels' worship of God that human worship of God cannot be compared to it. Such complete adoration by the angels to God is seen in their acts of worship that trying to worship God almost seems hopeless and useless for a human. Yet, the greater prize for God is for a human, even with a little pretense and even imperfectly, to worship Him. Christ did not die for the angels. He only died for humans. (See Matthew 20:28; 1 Peter 1:18; 1 Timothy 2:6; Romans 3:25; 5:10; 2 Corinthians 5:18; Isaiah 53:6–12; 1 Peter 2:24; 1 John 2:2; Hebrew 2:9; 8–10; Colossians 1:20; John 12:31–32.) Still, the angels of God by His redemption were affected in a redemptive sense. When a human worships God, it becomes a thorn in Satan's side. It shows that Christ's redemptive work is working and accomplishing what it was done for—to redeem men and women from Satan.

Another attribute of the angels is their ability to praise the Lord

God. So not only do angels worship the Lord God, but also praise Him. However, this praise done by the angels directed toward God is not localized, but universal in scope and degree. (See Revelation 4:8; Psalm 148:2; Isaiah 6:1–7; Luke 2:13; Job 38:7.) It echoes throughout the creation of God, even in the very kingdom of Satan, and even on earth where the struggle between God and Satan is especially ongoing. Such power is found in them praising the Lord God, that it shakes the earth back and forth. Satan is silenced. It affects all humanity and causes it to feel the pressure of Holy God. It causes all of humanity to repent and turn from their wicked ways. The very shaking of Satan's kingdom is seen. The very destruction of satanic powers in an area is manifested. The very power of God being manifested in creation is seen. The very knowledge and recognition that God hears prayers are manifested. The very assurance that God helps His saints is manifested. Also, the very assurance that God will supply His saints with strength and power to fight all battles that must be fought is manifested. The very acknowledgment that God will deal with what a saint asks for through His word, by justice, grace, and mercy, is also brought to the forefront.

The praise initiated by the angels to God is beyond human perception and actions just like the worship initiated by angels. The praise of the angels can be as singing, praying, or just speaking words of praise without any intention of forming it into singing or praying.

In Pseudo-Philo 19:16, it is recorded that the angels praise God with hymns. According to this book, the only time that the angels stopped praising God with hymns was when Moses died. However, notice that the prayers of the saints are seen to silence praise in heaven, when given unto God. (See Revelation 8:1–3.)

CHAPTER 6

Angelic Attributes Less Known

Angels Are Not Demons

IN ACTS 28:8–9, most differences between the Pharisees and Sadducees are brought to the forefront. Overall, the Pharisees believed that:

- ◆ there would be a resurrection,

- ◆ the soul is immortal from its creation,

- ◆ there would be a final judgment and eradication,

- ◆ the righteous will be imperishable,

- ◆ the wicked will endure everlasting punishment in fire that is unquenchable.

- ◆ angels were not demons.

Undoubtedly, the Pharisees were uniformly more favorable to be inclined with the doctrines of Christianity than the Sadducees. The Sadducees were almost considered atheists by other Jews, since they denied all these fundamental doctrines of Judaism that the Pharisees held as true. The Sadducees maintained that a man's destiny is in his own hands. On the other hand, the Pharisees clung to the conviction that the political relations with foreign nations are under the immediate control of the Holy One of Israel.

The Sadducees rejected the oral law of the Jewish people and rejected all the Old Testament, except the Pentateuch. Across from the fact that the Pharisees and Sadducees had vastly different opinions in what they believed in, there were very little differences among the other sects found in Judaism.

From an extensive search on the belief of demons, the Jewish people held that demons were something else than angels, whether unfallen or fallen. The belief that angels were the same things as demons was not derived from the Jewish people and their views at all, but from the heathen. Most of the heathen saw that the terms *angels* and *demons* are just different words meaning the same thing. This opinion so overwhelmed the heathen world that the view that angels and demons were not the same thing was thought strange.

In other words, the universal belief of Jews is that demons are not angels. The Jews held in one voice that demons have experienced physical death, and that the demons are at least male and female spirits.[1] The Jews held, as a rule, that the rebellion of Satan occurred before the advent of humanity. There are at least ten different Jewish interpretations on what demons are. All these theories retained the basic view that demons in their original state originated from the earth and not heaven. None state that they are fallen angels. The greatest Jewish interpretation is that demons are races before the advent of humanity. This interpretation predates the time of Ezra and the great Sanhedrin. In sources which support this idea it is said that demons were created long before man came into existence. They were the inhabitants of the earth and its masters. Dry land and sea were alike full of demons that lived happily for ages in peace and tranquility. For the whole planet was their domain. They were obedient and did the bidding of the Lord. Nevertheless, a day came when wickedness and evil deeds were found among all the demons, and they ignored the commandments of the Creator, and earth was full of their iniquity. With this, all of them followed Satan in his plan to destroy God and take over God's kingdom. And all the demons, suffered physical death, became disembodied spirits, accused of God, and destined to be thrown into hell.[2] This view is known as the Pre-Adamite Age.

Not all heathens accepted that angels and demons are the same. If the reader looks into the work of Hesiod, entitled *Works and Days*, the reader would find a belief similar to that proposed by the Jews. Hesiod wrote:

> First of all the immortals, who possess the mansion of Olympus, made a golden race of articulate-speaking men. These lived in the time of Gronos, when he ruled in heaven. Like gods they spent their lives, with hearts void of care, apart and altogether free from toils and trouble. Nor did miserable old age threaten them; but ever alike strong in hands and feet they rejoiced in festal pleasures far from the reach of all ills. And they died as if overcome by sleep. All blessings were theirs. And spontaneously the fruitful soil would bear crops great and abundant. And so they occupied their cultivated lands in tranquility and peace with many goods, being rich in flocks and dear to the blessed gods. But after that earth had covered this generation, they indeed by the counsels of mighty Zeus became demons, kindly ones, haunting the earth, being guardians of mortal men. These I ween, shrouded in mist, and going to and fro everywhere upon the earth, watch both the decisions of justice and harsh deeds, and are dispensers of riches. Such a royal prerogative is theirs.[3]

The original view of the early church on demons consisted of four basic elements:

- Demons once possessed physical bodies.
- Demons sinned and rebelled against God.
- Demons died a physical death.
- Demons lost their physical bodies and became disembodied spirits.[4]

From these basic elements, the earliest Christians conceived that demons were not angels, but the creatures of God created for the earth that rebelled against Him. The early church rejected that Satan created demons. Only God can create. (See John 1:3; Colossians 1:16; Ecclesiastes 3:11; Nehemiah 9:6; Psalm 148:2–6.) Demons were not created evil, but holy and good. They became evil due to their own wills and choice. It must be known that the demonology of the New Testament was derived from Judaism. This statement has been proven and dogmatically asserted.[5] Due to this, demons cannot be considered angels (whether unfallen or fallen) in the New Testament.

The first man to confess that angels were demons within the early church was Tatian, 110–172 A.D. Heathenism heavily influenced Tatian. This influence was so great that he fell from grace and became a reprobate. He formed his own Gnostic cult. His thinking about angels and demons was heathen throughout, in that he combined the two. His chief heresy was that Adam was not saved. Irenæus highly attacked this view.[6]

It was the consensus of the early church that the doctrine of Origen about angels becoming either men or demons was heretical. This was the case, so much so, that the early church officially condemned his teaching under the Second Council of Constantinople.[7] The early church had a strong opinion about angels not being demons. In this case, it was seen as heresy to say that demons and angels are the same.

The view that states that angels are not demons is also revealed in Acts 23:6–8 when Paul proclaims that he is a son of a Pharisee and that he holds the doctrine of the Pharisees. Since the Pharisees and all the sects of Judaism, except the Sadducees, accepted that there was a difference between angels and demons, then Paul himself believed this too. All his life, he had been taught the doctrines discussed in Acts 23 and the fact that fallen angels are not demons. The opponents to the view that angels and demons are different always point to the word "both" in Acts 23:8, which they say means that Paul meant only two subjects. The two subjects are the resurrection and the existence of spirits or angels. In other words, the opponents understand that both can only have reference to two subjects, and those subjects being the doctrine of the resurrection and the existence of spirits or angels. By this way of thinking, the nouns *spirit* and *angel* are assumed in this verse to refer to the same class of spiritual beings—angels. However, studying the Greek language, the word *both* comes from the Greek adjective ἀμφότερος (ämphŏtĕrōs). This Greek adjective does not necessarily mean "both." It can well mean "all," or "all together." Here it must mean "all" or "all together." Consequently, Acts 23:8 shows that three subjects are meant: the resurrection, angels, and spirits (demons). Then, it separates angels from demons and proves that angels are not the same thing as demons.

The Greek grammatical construction of Acts 23:8 shows that there are three direct subjects of the infinitive εἶναι (ēnĕ), and not two. Accordingly, angels and spirits in this verse are seen as separate and distinct subjects.

Further, demons are excluded from the term "angel" and from being spiritual beings. Why? Notice that one is called a spiritual being because one has a spiritual form that can materialize physically. One is called a physical being because of having a physical form. Demons are beings that lost their physical forms and entered the spiritual realm as disembodied spirits. Spiritual beings have spiritual natures while demons still are recognized as having physical natures due to having at one time physical bodies, but living in a disembodied state.

Christ Himself recognized the distinction between angels and demons, by stating that saints have authority over serpents and scorpions, in Luke 10:19. Christ declares that the saints do not have one enemy, but two. The serpents in Luke 10:19 represent fallen angels. What identifies the serpents as fallen angels is that Satan himself is called a serpent. (See Revelation 12:9, 14–15; 20:2.) The scorpions in Luke 10:19 represent demons. Demons are also described as scorpions in Revelation 9:3–10.

In Revelation 9, fallen angels and demons are clearly contrasted. A fallen angel is seen to be ruling over demons, which are like locusts in Revelation 9:11, while four fallen angels are seen ruling over demons with demons looking like horses and others looking like men in Revelation 9:13–17. It is stated very firmly that the rightful place for the demons is right now in the abyss, while the rightful place for fallen angels is in the Lake of Fire. (See Luke 8:31; Revelation 9:1–21.) The very distinction found in this shows that demons and fallen angels have not the same origin. While the rightful place for demons is now in the abyss, they like all rebels will be finally thrown into the Lake of Fire. (See Matthew 25:30–46; Revelation 14:9–11; 19:20.)

A very careful study of the phrases *spirits of demons* and *spirits of just men* prove that demons suffered physical death due to the rebellion of Satan and cannot be angels since angels cannot suffer physical death. (See Revelation 16:4; Hebrews 12:23.) Nowhere are angels called "spirits of angels," signifying that they suffered physical death and live in a disembodied state like the human dead do. Notice that the term *spirits of just men* mean that these men suffered death, live in a disembodied state, and are presently in heaven. (See James 2:26; Revelation 1:18; Luke 16:26–31; Ephesians 4:8–10; Hebrews 12:23; Revelation 6:9–11; 1

Kings 17:21–22; 2 Corinthians 5:8.) The comparison of these phrases, as understood in Greek grammar, underscores that demons were physical beings, suffered physical death, and due to suffering physical death are disembodied. Because demons are disembodied, they seek possession of physical bodies to try to indirectly obtain at least temporarily and partly, what they have lost. (See Mark 5:10; Matthew 4:24; 7:22; 8:16, 28–33; 9:32–33; 10:8; 12:22; 15:22; 17:18, 24–28.) In the Greek language, the *genitive* used is known as *genitive of inalienable possession.* This denotes that the spirits mentioned are an intrinsic part of the nature of both men and demons, but not the whole part at all. It states also that a part has been separated from the whole and that part is a physical body.

Mark 5:10 deals with demons not wanting to go outside their country. They hoped that Jesus would permit them not to enter a place outside their territory that they had been in for so long. The Greek noun χώρα (khōrä), commonly "country," literally means here a land that one has lived in before death, or a place that one has been given authority or power over before death. These meanings show four basic things: first, that these demons at once lived in the same place that they were operating in as physical beings; second, these demons tasted death, and by tasting death became disembodied spirits; third, these demons by knowing the land which they had lived in before death were given charge over it to do all their evil works therein; fourth, these demons are the disembodied spirits of those who lived before Adam. Dr. Wuest (a noted Greek Scholar) on Mark 5:10 writes:

> The request shows that demons at one time had physical bodies, for they have no rest unless they are in some physical body, either that of a human being, or that of an animal.[8]

Likewise, in Matthew 17:21 and Mark 9:29, Christ calls demons by the Greek noun γένος (yēnōs), which literally means "race." If demons are fallen angels, then they cannot be known as this Greek noun. Angels are not a race and a class, but only a class. This is firm proof that angels are not demons. Demons are races of beings other than the human race.

Moreover, when the fallen angels are mentioned in the New Testament, they are only mentioned in the masculine gender. The Greek noun for angels is in the masculine gender, and there is no way in Greek that angels can be seen as anything else, but masculine in gender. However, the

Greek points unshakably that the demons are sexless—without sex, masculine and feminine. This is seen from the two Greek nouns for demons being used in different genders. One noun being used in one gender, and the other being masculine or feminine.

In Isaiah 34:14, the prophet Isaiah mentions Lilith who was and is a female demon. Lilith is a proper name found in Hebrew and has been mistranslated from a screech owl to a monster. This is inconceivable since the Hebrew demands that this noun deals with a female demon.

In dealing with the origin of demons, it has been too easily overlooked that Satan ruled over the earth and over an ancient civilization—a Pre-Adamite society—who inhabited the earth ages before Adam. All these creatures rebelled, suffered physical death, and became the evil servants of Satan. (See Isaiah 14:12–15; Psalm 104:5–9; 2 Peter 3:5–7; Ezekiel 28:12–19; Genesis 1:2; 136:6; Matthew 13:35; 25:34; Mark 5:10.) Demons will regain bodily life in the resurrection. (See 1 Corinthians 15:44–49.) Anyone who denies a Pre-Adamite creation must explain in another way the origin of evil and the fall of Satan. Without this knowledge the origin of evil and the fall of Satan are incomplete and many answers are never forthcoming in many areas. In the next book on angels I will illuminate on Genesis 1:2 and the question of whether it has three circumstantial clauses.

One division of the early church also held to a belief that a Pre-Adamite creation had been created before Adam.[9] A division of the early church accepted this while interpreting Romans 5:12–14 and 1 Corinthians 15:21 in such as way as to still understand a Pre-Adamite creation. These verses are used to refute this. However, Greek thought demands that both death and sin entered the world of Adam as a force when Adam sinned. Before this, both death and sin had to exist so this could occur. Due to restoration, sin and death were destroyed upon the earth, not throughout creation.

The Four Arguments That Fallen Angels Are Demons Are Easily Overturned

1. Since Satan literally entered Judas Iscariot, then he must have been disembodied and as such a demon. (See Luke 22:3; John 13:27.) If Satan is a demon, then his angels are demons.

This is inconceivable because angels, whether fallen or unfallen, have spiritual bodies that cannot be separated from them. (See Judges 6:11;

1 Corinthians 15:44; Hebrews 13:1; Daniel 10:5–7; Genesis 18; 19; 1 Chronicles 21: 12–30.) Death cannot destroy their bodies, which are spiritual. Then, angels cannot become disembodied. Their forms are immortal. To be disembodied, one must have a spiritual part and a physical part. The physical part must die physically, so that the spiritual and physical parts can be separate in death. Angels have a spiritual nature, not a physical nature. Angels are immortal in form and cannot lose their bodily form. (See Matthew 22:30; Luke 20:35–36; Mark 12:25; Daniel 4:37.)

The second problem with this argument is that Scripture interprets scripture. John 13:2 interprets Luke 22:3 and John 13:27, defining what is meant. The entering into Judas by Satan actually was the act of Satan putting into the heart of Judas to betray Jesus.

The third problem is found in the Greek text of Luke 22:3 and John 13:27. The Greek verb εἰσέρχομαι (ēsěrkhōmě) in reference to Satan entering Judas literally means not a literal entrance of Satan into Judas, but Satan entering into agreement with Judas about Jesus. There is a meeting of the minds as it were, and Judas had accepted what Satan wanted. Satan had entered into alliance with Judas, and Judas submitted to this, allowing all of this willingly.

> 2. The term "the devil and his angels" are all inclusive, and demands that the angels here mentioned are demons. (See Matthew 25:41; Revelation 12:7.)

This is not true. Satan may be mentioned with any of his evil forces, whether that be his angels, demons, or wicked men. (See Matthew 12:24; Matthew 25:41; Luke 22:3.) Demons and fallen angels are different types of beings, and each deal with different orders and different areas of dominion within the kingdom of Satan.

> 3. Satan is known as "Beelzebub the prince of demons." (See Matthew 12:24.) Since Satan is the prince over the demons, then he must be one of these demons.

The Greek does not state that Satan is a demon, but only over them. In the Greek text, the *genitive of superiority* is used. This first means literally that Satan is superior to the demons in nature. If Satan were a demon, then his nature would be the same nature as that of the demons.

However, this cannot be the case. This Greek construction also demands that Satan is superior to demons in the realm of existence and origin. The *genitive of superiority* also establishes that Satan is superior to them in rank, position, power, authority, state, character, condition, influence, and other things. The *genitive of superiority* demands that Satan is not a demon, nor that demons are actually angels.

> 4. The demon locusts have a king over them. (See Revelation 9:1–11.) This view holds that this king is Satan. Therefore, the demons are fallen angels.

Notice that in verse 11 there appears the *genitive of superiority*. This construction denotes the same thing here as found in Matthew 12:24. There is no way that the demons here mentioned are fallen angels. The *genitive of superiority* denies that.

Giants, Not Demons

It is inconceivable that the giants, the Nephilim or Rephaim, are demons. (See Genesis 6:1–4.) Though this theory was widely known and accepted, it cannot be seen as fact. Its acceptance may have been due to a fact that certain passages of Scripture were not studied or known. All the evidence was not expounded.

Demons were in existence before the event of Genesis 6 as already noted. The giants were the offspring of an unholy mixture of fallen angelic nature and fallen human nature. They are cursed and have no resurrection. (See Isaiah 14:9; 26:14; Proverbs 2:18; 9:18; 21:16), while all ordinary men are to be resurrected. (See John 5:28–29.) Isaiah 26:14 reads, "They are dead, They shall not live; they, the Rephaim, are deceased, they shall not rise…" Scripture is also clear that the Rephaim are in Sheol-Hades—not the bottomless pit—awaiting judgment and cannot be the demons. Isaiah 14:9 reads, "Sheol from beneath is moved for you to meet you at your coming: it stirreth up the Rephaim for you, *even* all the chief ones of the earth; it hath raised up from their thrones all the kings of the nations." Proverbs 21:16 reads, "The man that wandereth out of the way of understanding shall rest in the assembly of the Rephaim." Proverbs 9:18 reads, "But he knoweth not that the Rephaim are there; and that her guests are in the depths of hell." Proverbs 2:16 reads from the

Greek Septuagint, "For she has fixed her house near death, and *guided* her wheels near Hades with the giants." Ezekiel 32:27 reads from the Greek Septuagint, "And they are laid with the giants that fell of old, who went down to Hades with *their* weapons of war...."

Angels Are Males

Whenever an angel usually appeared in the Old Testament and New Testament, the appearance was very much that of a man. For this reason, angels were often mistaken for men and referred to as man. (See Genesis 18:2,18; 19; Daniel 8; 9; Judges 13:6–11; Revelation 21:17; Ezekiel 9:2.) However, some angels like the Ofannim and three groups of the Cherubim have not the appearance like a man. Yet they are masculine.

The Greek and Hebrew languages are so clear about the angels being male that it cannot be easily doubted. Some declare that it means nothing when angels are spoken of as males. Does it mean nothing also for God the Father, God the Word, and God the Holy Spirit? Christ did not appear as a female or a thing, but as a male. According to natural law, the human male determines the gender of any offspring produced by natural conception. However, without the human male the offspring produced through the incarnation, as concerning the humanity of Christ, should have been a daughter rather than a son. Where did the masculine aspect come from? The gender of the divine nature determined the gender of the human nature of Christ.[10] One cannot delete from the Bible the masculine aspect of God without distorting the Bible.

Certain passages of Scripture do not prove that God is sexless. (See Isaiah 42:14; Deuteronomy 4:15–20.) For example, Isaiah 42:14 only depicts God as giving a loud cry, a roar, or an outcry like a woman in birth at the Second Coming. This very idea does not show that God is sexless or a woman. Men act on occasions like women and women like men, and this does not show that they are sexless. What God is attempting to show here is His utter readiness to cause the Second Coming.

Masculine pronouns are only used for angels. (See Revelation 7:2; 8:3; 9:3; 10:2–11; 20:1–3; Acts 12:7–8; Daniel 8:14–19; 9:22; 10:11–20; 12:7–9; Exodus 23:21; Judges 6:13–15; Genesis 16:7–8; 22:11–12.)

The belief that angels were not masculine, but sexless, or female, was not conceived until the fourth century A.D. Before that date, all

Jewish scholars and Christian scholars affirmed that the Scriptures demand that all angels are males. The change of thought was for four reasons: angels in the fourth century were overly spiritualized to the point that they were being worshiped as only God should be worshiped, the dominance of the allegorical method of interpretation, the institution of celibacy for clergy, and the desire to undermine the universal belief that the "sons of God" in Genesis 6:1–4 were undeniably fallen angels, committing fornication, as witnessed in Jude 6–7. Angels are called "sons of God" in Job 1:6, 2:1. They are never called the "women of God" or the "things of God."

The Jews of antiquity believed that the angels of God were circumcised, and this circumcision was a sign that they were in covenant with God. On this account, the angels could participate with Israel in all of their rites and feasts including the Sabbath. (See Jubilees 15:27.) This belief also went further about fallen angels. It is affirmed that the fallen angels, having broken their covenant with God, sought to signify this in many ways, one being to uncircumcise themselves. It is quite interesting that the many Jews during the times of Antiochus IV so abandoned the Lord and His covenant that they sought artificially to remove the traces of ever being circumcised. (See 2 Maccabees 4:11–17; 1 Maccabees 1:11–15; Assumption of Moses 8:1–5.)

So predominant in antiquity was the belief that angels leaving their spiritual realm had the ability as males to produce offspring by women of humanity that it overwhelms the study of angels. In Judges 13:6, 9, the angel is not called the "woman of God" or the "thing of God," but the "man of God."

Angels Are Not Humans

In Hebrews 2:16, it clearly states that angels and humans are different. There are many differences between angels and humans:

- Angels are of a different nature than that of humans.

- Christ did not take upon Himself the nature of angels, but the nature of humans.

- Angels are spiritual beings while humans are physical beings.

- Angels have a spiritual nature while humans have a physical nature.

- Angels are seen to be higher than humans. (See Psalm 8:3–8; 1 Corinthians 14:32.)

- If angels were humans, then why will Christ confess the names of the overcomers to the angels? (See Luke 12:8; Revelation 3:5.)

- Angels can override the laws of nature, in accordance to the will of God, while humans cannot.

- Angels are sent to minister to the heirs of eternal and unconditional salvation. The angels are not the heirs. The heirs are redeemed humans. (See Hebrews 1:14.)

- Humans cannot be considered countless in number like angels. (See Hebrews 12:22; Revelation 5:11.)

- Saints will rule over angels. (See 1 Corinthians 6:3.) If angels were humans, then this could not be.

- Angels were already created when God created the earth in order of creation, not in time of creation. (See Job 38: 6–7.)

- Christ comes with angels and saints at the Second Coming. If the angels were humans, then there would be only angels.

- In Luke 16:22–25, the angels are seen as separate from the spirits of the departed saints.

- Humans cannot move from the physical realm to the spiritual realm at will or from the spiritual realm to the physical realm. (See Genesis 18:1–19; 2 Kings 19:35; Acts 12:7.)

- In Hebrews 12:22–23, angels are seen as separate from the church and all spirits of just men. Therefore, angels are not only distinct from the humans that make up the church, but also all spirits of just men found in heaven who are part of the community of saints.

- Angels are not a race, but only a class of spiritual beings. (See Hebrews 2:16; 12:22; Luke 20:34–36.) Humans are a class and a race.

- Angels were created simultaneously while humans are not.

- In Matthew 22:30, Luke 20:35, and Mark 12:25, the saints in the resurrection are only considered like the nature of angels in certain things. As a result, humans are not seen to be angels, but only like them.

- The angelic nature is the highest and most exalted created nature. Yet, God is pleased to put greater honor upon the human nature, which is inferior, by causing the Head and King of the creation to come down and become man.

- God the Father is not considered a Father to the angels while God the Father is considered a Father to the saints.

- Angels cannot die physically. (See Matthew 22:30; Luke 20:35–36; Mark 12:25; Daniel 4:37) while humans can. (See Hebrews 9:27; Genesis 3:7–19; James 2:26.)

Angels Do Not Marry

In Matthew 22:30, Luke 20:35–36, and Mark 12:25, Christ does not say that at the resurrection men will become angels. Rather, Christ says that at the resurrection men will be as angels or equal unto the angels in certain things. As a result, the view that all angels were once human cannot be the truth. The main point of these verses is that in the life that comes after the resurrection, men will be as the angels of God in heaven now are, immortal in body, and without need of marriage to propagate their kind.

In 2 Baruch, it is said that the righteous will be made like unto the angels. (See 2 Baruch 51:10.) In addition, 1 Enoch 15:6–7 states that the reason God did not make wives for angels is simply because wives were made for the human race, and not for spiritual beings in heaven.

Angels not marrying or being given in marriage does not mean that they are sexless. It simply means that they need not replenish their kind since they are immortal. This is what Christ was trying to get across. Luke

20:35–36 gives the same reason in the statement, "…neither can they die any more."

The fact that the angels of God, who are not sexless, do not marry each other in heaven is also seen to be because all angels are males. Still, this fact does not deter the belief that fallen angels have left the spiritual realm and cohabited with human women. Fallen angels did do all these things. (See Genesis 6:1–4; 2 Peter 2:4–6; Jude 5–7.) The fact that fallen angels have done all these things signifies that angels out of their habitation, which is the spiritual realm, do have the power to reproduce. However, this act is forbidden, and the fallen angels that did this are suffering for it. None of the unfallen angels will ever do this, since no hint of sin is found in them.

In Matthew 22:30, Luke 20:35–36, and Mark 12:25, the Greek verb γάμεω (gämĕō) means that the angels do not enter the state of marriage in heaven. The Greek verb γαμίζω (gämĕzō) in these verses means "to be permitted to marry." Therefore the full content of these verses is that angels do not enter the state of marriage in heaven neither are they permitted to marry in heaven. The fact that marriage is not permitted in heaven is a clear reference to the belief that there is no female angel in heaven or any other place. Only on the earth is marriage found. This is another reason angels do not marry or are not permitted to marry because marriage is an institution provided for the earth and not for the heavens.

Angels Travel at Very Fast Speeds

According to Scripture, angels apparently can travel at very fast speeds to the point that these speeds are inconceivable to the human minds. (See Daniel 4:13; Isaiah 6:1–7; Revelation 9:11.) It can be imagined that angels travel at very slow speeds. It can even be imagined that angels travel at the speed of sound or light. However, it is very hard to imagine angels traveling at faster speeds such as the speed of thought. The speed of thought means that as fast as the angel can think of being in a place, he is there.

These spiritual beings travel at this speed to achieve the purposes and will of God throughout His kingdom and even in Satan's kingdom. Why cannot the speed of thought be understood? Angels have minds that are not clouded with fleshly desires, nor are their minds clouded with anything that would disable them in thinking. Therefore, their minds work in a greater and faster mode than human minds. Really their minds work so fast that humans just cannot comprehend it. If a human could travel at the speed of thought, it would not be the same speed of travel that the angels can achieve. For if a human could travel to a place by the speed of thought, an angel would have already thought of going to that place and have already been there for several months or years waiting for a human to show up.

Angels do not always travel at the speed of thought. They can travel at the speed of light, the speed of sound, or even slower. Angels who have wings can use their wings to travel. (See Isaiah 6:1–7.) Angels who have wings do not have to use them to travel for they also have the ability of traveling by the speed of thought.

The wings are a tangible method of travel. Traveling without wings is an intangible method of travel. When angels use wings there is an outward manifestation upon his person that he is traveling in this fashion. His wings will begin to move back and forth causing him to move wherever he wants, which shows outward motion. When angels do not use wings to travel, there is no outward manifestation upon his person that he is traveling. Nothing is moving upon his person. This shows no outward motion upon his person. This power is intangible.

The Seraphim, second, third, and fourth groups of the Cherubim, and the chief angels are the only angels who have wings. The first group of Cherubim in their order, and the other orders do not have wings. In Ezekiel 10:12, the term *wings* concerning the Ofannim does not mean wings, but "tongues" as already mentioned.

The angels of God travel at fast speeds for various reasons. For example, the vastness of the heavenlies requires them to travel at unbelievable speeds in order to do God's will and to defend God's kingdom. They are swifter than anything physical. No physical boundary can hinder their travel.

Angels Can Ascend and Descend at Will

In Genesis 28:10–12 Jacob had a dream. In this dream, he saw a stairway set up on the earth and the top of it reached God's heaven. As he was seeing this stairway, he suddenly saw the angels of God ascending and descending upon it with the Lord God standing above the stairway.

The most important part of Genesis 28:11–12 is verse 12. In verse 12, Jacob is said to have seen not a ladder, but a stairway. From both the Greek Septuagint and the Masoretic Hebrew text, the idea is so clear that the stairway was not any longer upon the earth but had been pulled up. Though the stairway is permanently affixed in heaven, the stairway is not permanently fixed to a certain part of the earth.

Genesis 28:13 shows that the stairway was still firmly and permanently attached to a place in heaven while the stairway on the earth had been pulled up and was no more upon the earth at that time. Why? The stairway is lifted up from the earth when angels are in the midst of ascending to heaven. The stairway is lowered down to the earth and again affixed to the place that God so designs it to be at a given time only when angels are in the midst of descending to the earth. The very fact that Jacob saw the stairway being affixed on the earth shows that certain angels were in the midst of descending and only after they had descended completely to the earth would God allow other angels to begin their ascent to heaven.

One must recognize that the stairway, to Jacob, was a visible manifestation of God's fellowship with man. The ascending of the angels is seen to be more important than descending. Why? The ascending of the angels is an indication that the mission of the angels, whatever it might be, is accomplished for the saints. The descending of the angels is an indication that the angels' mission, whatever it might be, is not yet accomplished, but only beginning. So, the ascending signifies the completion of a mission and the availability to begin another while the descending signifies that the angels are only beginning their mission. This reason is also found in John 1:51.

Further, the angels ascending on the stairway carry up the wants and desires of God's people in prayer form. The angels descending on the stairway carry back answers to prayers, assistance, and protection from the world, Satan, and his forces.

Does this stairway to heaven still exist? Yes! According to the Jews and their point of view about this whole dream, Jacob was shown the conditional course of the world's history and the part that angels have had and will have in it. Jacob not only saw many angels ascending and descending, but in particular the angels that would be the satanic chief angels over the four kingdoms mentioned in Daniel 2 and Daniel 7. According to the Jews, all other loosed fallen angels, beside satanic chief angels, can use this stairway on certain occasions to ascend to heaven and descend from it, and on occasions, demons can use this stairway too. When the forces of evil use this stairway to ascend to heaven and to descend from it, they are going to and coming back from a heavenly conference meeting that transpires in the throne room of God. (See 1 Kings 22:19; Job 1:6; 2:1; Matthew 18:10.)

Secondly, Jacob was shown in a conditional sense the revelation at Mount Sinai, the translation of Elijah, the Temple in its glory and desolation, and Nebuchadnezzar and his attempt to burn the three Hebrew children. Of course, the stairway is not the only way for the forces of God and the forces of evil to reach heaven and the throne of God. However, it is one very special way. For in this way, the angels and the forces of evil do not have to show any effort of motion. According to Hebrew and Greek meaning, the stairway is similar to an escalator. The stairway is stationed in heaven in the very throne room of God.

The stairway is a direct way to travel to the throne of God and God Himself. The stairway cannot be a symbol of Christ. Why? The stairway is a literal path from the earth to heaven that will literally take one to heaven, the throne room of God, and God Himself.

In John 1:51, Christ seems to tell Nathanael, that is, Bartholomew, alone that he will see heaven opened and angels ascending and descending upon Christ. The Greek verb ὁράω (ōräō) explicitly means that Nathanael would truly see a vision of heaven opened and the angels ascending and descending upon Christ.

The problem with many interpretations of this verse is the fact that many symbolize away that Nathanael would see heaven opened and angels ascending and descending upon the Son of Man. This does untold harm to what Christ was telling Nathanael. Christ promised Nathanael that he would see heaven opened and angels ascending and descending upon the Son of Man.

However, this promise was not to Nathanael alone. The Greek verb used is found in the second person plural *future tense*. This shows that the "you" is not referring only to Nathanael, but to others who will see the same thing that Nathanael shall see. Who are these others? The other apostles. These were also at the ascension of Christ. This gives credence to the view that Nathanael was none other than an apostle of Christ, Bartholomew. What Nathanael sees, the other apostles shall see simultaneously. Therefore, it must refer to the ascension when all the apostles, except Judas, saw Christ ascend to heaven, heaven opened, and the angels ascending and descending through Christ.

At the ascension, heaven was literally opened, which symbolized that the assistance and grace of the Lord God are forever present now. An opened heaven is a symbol of the assistance and grace of the Lord God. (See Genesis 28:10–17; Isaiah 6:1; Malachi 3:10; 1 Kings 8:35; Acts 7:17; 10:11.) A closed heaven is an expression that signifies the absence of assistance and grace of the Lord God with and impending judgment replacing it. (See Isaiah 64:1.)

The very fact that Christ declares that Nathanael and the other Apostles will see heaven opened shows that heaven before Christ was closed to man. Nevertheless, with Christ coming this changed, and heaven is freely given access to humanity by Christ. (See John 14:6.)

On that account, complete and uninterrupted relationship between God and man is initiated through Christ only. Before the fall, complete and uninterrupted relationship between God and man was assured, not after that. The fall destroyed this kind of relationship between God and man.

The statement that angels of God are ascending and descending upon the Son of man must also be taken in a broader sense. It must be taken in the sense that Christ alone is the way through which the angels can minister to the saints. Angels ascend and descend through Christ to minister to the saints. As such, the angels descend from Christ to the earth and ascend back up to Him, signifying that Christ is the source of their beginning and their end in ministry at a particular time and place.

This connects John 1:51 with Genesis 28:11–12. The divine person who appeared to Jacob in a dream was none other than Christ in His preincarnate state. Christ saying this shows that He will again be the source of the angels' ministry at His ascension. In His voluntary subordinate state upon the earth, Christ was not the source since Christ in this state gave up all authority over angels, being a man totally. How was this done? He gave up the free use of His divine power and authority by His own will being lowered for the sake of humanity. (See Philippians 2:6–7; Hebrews 1:1–2:18; Matthew 26:53.)

Therefore, by Christ's redemptive work, heaven is now open permanently. Angels now permanently ascend and descend as faithful servants, teachers, prophets, guardians, and messengers between God and man, and, in particular, between God and the saints. Before Christ's death, heaven being opened was only temporarily done and that occurred because of Christ's appearance upon the earth and His ministry in His pre-incarnate state. Yet, it took Christ's completed redemptive work to keep it permanently open for all eternity.

The angels ascending and descending to minister to the heirs of eternal and unconditional salvation through Christ as their source only officially began again at the ascension of Christ that took place in front of the apostles and others as confirmed in Acts 1:9.

Angels Are Immortal

From Matthew 22:30, Luke 20:35–36, and Mark 12:25, it is known that at the resurrection men will be as angels are, immortal. Luke 20:35–36 states, "neither can they die any more." This again denotes that angels are immortal.

Angels Have Seats of Emotions and Knowing

Angels must have what can be called a seat of emotions (or feelings) and a seat of knowing. Both indicate that the angels have a personality. Accordingly, they have every feature that a person needs to have individuality. (See Numbers 22:22–35; 2 Peter 2:10–11; Jude 8–9.)

Angels are seen to have a seat of emotions. Here is a partial list of attributes which indicate this fact:

1. Anger (Rev. 12:12)
2. Appetites (Gen. 18:8)
3. Lusts (John 8:44)
4. Enmity (Gen. 3:15)
5. Emotions (Luke 15:1–10)
6. Passions (Jude 6–7)
7. Vengeance (1 Pet. 5:8)
8. Desires (1 Pet. 1:12)
9. Grief (1 Cor. 11:10)
10. Pride (Ezek. 28:12–19)

Angels are seen to have a seat of knowing. Here is a partial list of attributes which indicate this fact:

1. Obedience (Matt. 26:53)
2. Intelligence (2 Sam.14:17)
3. Wisdom (2 Sam. 14:20)

4. Holiness (Luke 9:26)
5. Patience (Num. 22:22–35)
6. Knowledge (Mark 13:32)
7. Wills (Isa. 14:12–15)
8. Mind (Dan. 10:1–21)
9. Speak (1 Cor. 13:1)
10. Humility (2 Pet. 2:10–11)

The seat of emotions is also called the soul; the seat of knowing is also called the spirit. Therefore, angels have some type of inner man similar to that of humanity. In accordance, the angels are not only sentient beings but also free moral agents and rational beings. Notice that the term *soul* when used alone without the term *spirit* has reference many times to the whole inner man. This is also true of the term *spirit*.

This part like their whole being is immortal. What does this mean? From their creation, the angels will forever exist. (See Hebrews 11:13–16; 1 Peter 3:4; 4:6; Daniel 12:2–3; Luke 20:28; John 6:51; 10:28; 1 John 2:17; Matthew 12:40; Ephesians 4:7–11.)

Angels Have Spiritual Bodies

That the angels have bodies is clearly seen from the Scriptures. (See Judges 6:11; 1 Corinthians 15:44; Hebrews 13:1; Daniel 10:5–7; Genesis 18; 19.) Nowhere in Scripture does anyone find that angels are formless creatures without any type of form. Nowhere in Scripture does anyone find that angels are demons without bodies.

When studying angelic nature, one will become confronted with the belief by many that the angels are disembodied spirits. Often, the Higher Critics have rejected the whole section of theology known as Angelology simply because they cannot see how angels have spiritual bodies. The appearing of angels in absolute flesh to Abraham in the Old Testament shows that angels are not disembodied spirits, but bodied spirits. (See Genesis 18–19.)

The word *spirit* in Hebrew and Greek as they relate to angels refers to spiritual beings who possess spiritual bodies. When these words were used to describe angels by the ancients, they understood that these words did not deny that angels were endowed with spiritual bodies though their nature is spiritual. The ancients understood that the angels were intangible only in the sense that the angels were and are free from the impurities of gross and earthy matter and free from mortal organization of flesh.

The distinction between spiritual bodies and physical bodies spoken of by Paul in 1 Corinthians 15:44 shows that angels have spiritual bodies. In other words, the main difference between spiritual bodies and physical bodies is that spiritual bodies are adapted to that of the spiritual realm, and physical bodies are adapted to that of the physical realm. (See 1 Corinthians 15:44.) Only demons and the departed dead are bodiless. (See Luke 16:22; Revelation 16:13–16.)

If angels are bodiless, then their appearance in the physical realm would be impossible. Yet, angels have appeared in the physical realm before. (See Daniel 3:24–35; Genesis 18:2–33; 19:1–26.)

If angels are bodiless like demons, then the only way that angels could be manifested in the physical realm is by possessing a human like demons do. Yet, angels can make themselves known and be seen in the physical realm by appearing to men in tangible bodies. Their spiritual bodies accomplish this by transforming into physical bodies. (See Hebrews 13:1; Daniel 3:24b–35; Genesis 18:2–19:26.) Further, if angels were bodiless, then how could Gabriel fight against the satanic chief angel of the Medo-Persian Empire hand to hand in Daniel 10, unless each could see, touch, and hold each other in a fighting grasp? This fight was real, tangible, and physical.

The ability of angels to interact between the spiritual realm and the physical realm would be very limited if they did not have spiritual bodies. In fact, the ancients concluded that if the angels were without spiritual bodies that could be transformed into physical bodies, then there exists an unbridgeable gulf between the spiritual realm and the physical realm. Only in their eyes could this unbridgeable gulf stop existing if the angels have spiritual bodies.

Luke 24:37–39 states that a spirit has not bones and flesh. Therefore, Christ taught that angels have not bodies of flesh and bones. Still, Christ did not state that angels are bodiless, but only that their bodies are not made of flesh and bones.

According to Scripture, angels wear literal clothes. (See John 20:15; Revelation 15:6) Angels wear real and material clothes that can be touched and seen in the spiritual realm and can be transformed into real and material clothes in the physical realm. So, the clothes that angels wear are truly real.

Both demons and the departed dead do not have actual bodies, but have soulish forms. The soulish forms resemble the outward outline of the body and are themselves the outward outline of the soul. Demons and the departed dead are usually seen wearing clothes. Yet, since they are bodiless, they do not have real clothes on. What is seen is simply the form of their souls that cause themselves to be recognized as wearing clothes. For example, so great is this impression that an effect is produced upon the minds of those who can see demons that they think that the clothes are really present, but in reality all they are seeing is simply the outward outline of the demons fashioned to be seen in that manner. The body itself is a reflection of how the soul looks. The appearance of the soul will determine how the body looks. Irenæus also agrees with this view.[11]

These forms are seen to act much like bodies going through the appearance of doing things that only bodies can do. Yet, it is only an appearance. The forms cannot do what bodies can do, though it may seem like it. For example, if a demon sits down he, she, or it is not literally sitting down. A demon has nothing to sit down—no body. Demons and the human dead have only the appearance of sight, hearing, touch, smell, and taste. Though the actual senses are no longer carried out due to an absence of their bodies, through spiritual properties from their spirits they can imitate these senses.

An angel can only in a sense carry and hold a soul. A soul cannot be held or carried by an angel's hands. So does an angel do this? An angel, as with Lazarus, can carry a soul by his supernatural power. (See Luke 16:19–31.) In other words, the supernatural power of the angel is what holds the soul of the departed saint and carries it to heaven. It is this power in Old Testament times that carried the soul of the saint in paradise beneath the surface of the earth. The supernatural power of an angel totally surrounds, like a force field, the soul of a departed saint. By this method the angel can control where the soul is going.

It is an angel's supernatural power that enables him to grab hold of demons. Since demons are bodiless, an angel can only hold them by his power. His hand cannot grasp a demon, yet his power can. The supernatural power of an angel achieves this with demons in the same manner that it achieves this with the souls of the departed saints. The supernatural power of an angel totally surrounds a demon. It is by this that an angel can control where a demon is going and can defeat it in battle. A satanic angel cannot be fought in this fashion but must be fought against hand to hand. This type of fight is real, tangible, and physical in the spiritual realm. So, fighting against fallen angels is harder for God's angels fighting against demons.

In Matthew 22:30, Luke 20:35–36, and Mark 12:25, the idea of angels having spiritual bodies is well known. The saints will be like them. How? The bodies of the saints will be like the spiritual bodies that the angels have. The bodies of the saints will be flesh and bone though changed to be like spiritual bodies. The bodies of the angels do not consist of these elements.

The existence of a creation that is bodiless is next to impossible. The only exceptions are demons as they are now and the departed human dead. Yet, both demons and the departed human dead at one time had bodies. God never created anything without some kind of form.

The Babylonian Talmud teaches that an angel is not some kind of formless being, but has a spiritual body that is in some respects like the body of a man.[12] Also, the *Dead Sea Scrolls* teach that angels have spiritual bodies that can be transformed into physical bodies. The *Genesis Apocryphon* teaches that angels do have spiritual bodies that are capable to be transformed into physical bodies. The ancient church concluded that to be without bodily form is demonic, a divine penalty, or both.[13] It is essential for a spiritual being to have localized, determinate, and spiritual form.

All types of angels have a type of embodiment. (See Isaiah 6:1–7; Ezekiel 1:4–28; 1:11, 23; 3:13; 10; 11:22; 28:14–16; Revelation 4:6, 8, 9; 5:6, 8, 11, 14; 6:1, 6, 8; 7:11; 14:3; 15:7; 19:14.)

The belief that angels have some type of embodiment was always attacked by the heathens. Why? Gnosticism taught that all things which are of the body or which deal with the body are evil. Then, it was believed that the body was where evil came from. They saw any type of embodiment as evil and that includes spiritual bodies.

The universal belief of the early church before the fourth century was that angels have some type of embodiment. St. Augustine, an Early Church Father, states in his work entitled *Enchiridion*:

> Further, who will tell what sort of bodies it was that the angels appeared to men, making themselves not only visible, but tangible; and again, how it is that, not through material bodies, but by spiritual power, they present visions not to the bodily eyes, but to

the spiritual eyes of the mind, or speak something not into the ear from without, but from within the soul of the man, they themselves being stationed there too…or appeared to men in sleep, and make communications through dreams. For these methods of communications seem to imply that the angels have not tangible bodies, and make it a very difficult question to solve how the patriarchs washed their feet, and how it was Jacob wrestled with the angel in a way so unmistakably material.[14]

St. Augustine writes in his work entitled *The City of God:*

However, the same trustworthy scripture testifies that angels have appeared to men in such bodies as could not only be seen but also touched. There is, too, a very general rumor, which many have verified by their own experience, or which trustworthy persons who have heard the experience of others corroborate, that sylvans and fauns, who are commonly called "incubi," had often made wicked assaults upon women, and satisfied their lust upon them; and that certain devils called Duses by the Gauls, are constantly attempting and effecting this impurity is so generally affirmed that it was impudent to deny it.[15]

Tertullian, an Early Church Father, writes in his work entitled *Against Marcion:*

Now in this discussion of yours, when you suppose that we are to be met with the case of the Creator's angels, as if they held intercourse with Abraham and Lot in a phantom state, that of merely putative flesh, and yet did truly converse, and eat, and work, as they had been commissioned to do, you will not, to begin with, be permitted to use as examples the acts of that God whom you are destroying….But then, secondly you must know that it will not be conceded to you, that in the angels there was only a putative flesh, but one of a true and solid human substance. For if (on your terms) it was no difficulty to him to manifest true sensations and actions in a putative flesh, it was much more easy for him still to have assigned the true substance of flesh to these true sensations and actions, as the proper maker and former thereof….My God, however, who formed that which He had taken out of the dust of the ground in the true quality of flesh, although not issuing as yet from conjugal seed, was equally able to apply to angels too a flesh of any material whosoever, who built even the world out of nothing, into so many and various bodies, and that at a word!....It is more difficult for God to practice deception than to produce real flesh from any material whatever, even without the means of birth. But for other heretics, in addition, who maintain that the flesh in the angels ought to have been born of flesh, if it had been really human, we have an answer on a sure principle, to the effect that it was truly human flesh, and yet not born. It was truly human, because of the truthfulness of God, who can neither lie nor deceive, and because (angelic beings) cannot be dealt with by men in a human way except in human substance: it was withal unborn, because none but Christ could become incarnate by being born of the flesh in order that by his own nativity He might regenerate our birth, and might further by his death also dissolve our death, by rising again in that flesh in which that He might even die, He was born.[16]

Tertullian writes in his work entitled *On the Flesh of Christ:*

You have sometimes read and believed that the Creator's angels have been changed into human form, and have even borne about so veritable a body, that Abraham even washed their feet, and Lot was rescued from the Sodomites by their hands; an angel, moreover, wrestled with a man so strenuously with his body, that the latter desired to be let loose, so tightly was he held....Still there was solidity in their bodily substance, whatever may have been the force by which the body became visible. What is written cannot but have been.[17]

Tertullian in this same work writes again:

It is plain that the angels bore a flesh which was not naturally their own; their nature being of a spiritual substance, although in some sense peculiar to themselves, corporeal.[18]

John Cassian, an Early Church Father, writes in his work *First Conference of Abbot Serenus:*

For though we maintain that some spiritual natures exist, such as angels....yet we ought certainly not to consider them incorporeal. For they have in their own fashion of a body in which they exist, though it is much finer than our bodies are.[19]

95

Origen, an Early Church Father, in his work *De Principiis* writes:

> In which world certain beings are said to be super-celestial, i.e., placed in happier abodes, and clothed with heavenly and resplendent bodies.[20]

Angels Have Names

At the creation of the angels, God gave to each angel a personal name. God not only gave them each individuality, but confirmed it by giving each a personal name. Having a personal name helps establish that one has a personality and does exist.

Angels usually do not reveal their personal names to humans. This does, however, occasionally occur. (See Daniel 8:16; 9:21–23; 10:13, 21; 12:1; Luke 1:19, 26.) Why? Angelic cults were very common in antiquity and are seen in modern times. The appearance of an angel usually starts angelic cults with the giving of the name of that angel. It takes an appearance and usually the giving of the name of that angel to start an angelic cult. However, simply the appearance of an angel can start an angelic cult.

What is an angelic cult? Really, an angelic cult is an attempt by man to worship angels. But notice that an angelic cult worships not many gods, but one god, which is the one angelic nature in its various forms. According to Josephus, the Essenes kept a very well organized and extensive list of the names of angels.[21] The keeping of the list of the names of angels by the Essenes was done for one purpose. What was it? To worship those angels. As such, the Essenes kept this extensive list so that many angelic cults could be instigated by them for all these angels. The Essenes as a whole were turning from monotheism to a strange kind of polytheism and incorporating into their worship many angels.

Polytheism, when rightly defined, holds that there are many gods, who possess different natures, and who may or may not be united by will and purpose.

On the occasions that God allows His angels to reveal their personal names to individuals, God is showing that He trusts the saint. The Scriptures do not give details about the personal name of each angel. Yet, the Scriptures do give the various names that angels as a whole are called:

- "Spiritual beings" has reference to the nature of angels. (See Psalm 104:4.)

- "Hosts" has reference to the angels arranged into angelic armies. (See Genesis 32:1–2; 1 Kings 22:19–23.) The plural shows that they are many angelic armies. The term "hosts" is used as a name for angels in the Dead Sea scrolls. For example, this name is found in the *Book of Hymns* (Chapter 3, verse 35.)

- "Stars" has reference to the heavenly origin of the angels and their heavenly nature. (See Revelation 2–3; Job 38:7.)

- "Elect" has reference to the fact that after the rebellion of Satan those who did not rebel were chosen by the Lord and were confirmed by God as still being His holy angels. (See 1 Timothy 5:21.) So, God chose these angels as His holy messengers and rejected those angels who rebelled with Satan in original rebellion against God. (See Isaiah 14:12–15.) Before this awful rebellion, God had chosen all angels by creation as His holy messengers and ministers. Now, God has only chosen those angels who do not rebel against Him and are obedient. 1 Timothy 5:21 shows that the holy angels are set apart from the rebellious angels as the receivers and recipients of special favor and privilege because they did not rebel with Satan and his followers.

- "Saints" has reference to the holiness of angels. (See Psalm 89:5–7; Job 15:15.)

- "Assembly of gods" has reference to the angels' excellency and greatness in respect to humans and all other created beings. (See Psalm 82:1.) They are also called this because they are spiritual beings like God, but in an inferior way being created by God. While angels are like God in some respect, this is only in a very inferior manner and does not make them equal to God nor does it make them uncreated.

- "Angels" has reference to the class of spiritual beings. It defines that angels are spiritual beings. (See Psalm 104:4.)

- "Sons of God" has reference to the fact that angels were created in the likeness of God and that their creation is a direct divine-specific act of God done simultaneously without need of birth or other means of propagation. (See Job 1:6; 2:1; 38:7.) Also, the name "sons of God" denotes the same thing that the name "assembly of gods" does. In the Dead Sea scrolls, the angels are known as sons. For example, in the *Book of Hymns*, this name for angels is found. (See Chapter 3, verse 22.)

- "Ministers" has reference to the office of the angels. (See Psalm 104:4; 103:21.)

- "A flaming fire" has reference to the work of the angels. (See Psalm 104:4.)

- "Gods" means the same thing as "assembly of gods." (See Psalm 82:6.)

- "Mighty" has reference to the manifestation of God's power through them. (See Psalm 29:1.)

- "Men of God" has reference to the general appearance of many angels and their origin being from God. (See Judges 13:6–9.)

- "Men" has reference to the general appearance of many angels and their masculine gender. (See Genesis 18–19; Judges 13:6–9; Revelation 21:17.)

- "Angels of destruction" or "destroyers" has reference to God's angels usually employed by the Creator in judgments that bring forth punishment, destruction, or death. (See Exodus 12:23; Job. 20:15; 33:22–23; 36:14.) The terms *angels of destruction* and *destroyers* are also found in the Babylonian Talmud.[22] This term is also found in 1 Enoch 53:3, 56:1, 3 Enoch 31:1–2, and 33:1–2. It is even found in the Dead Sea scrolls in the book *The Manual of Discipline.*

- "Servants" has reference to God's angels giving obedience and servitude toward God. (See Revelation 22:8–9; 19:10.)

Angels Need No Rest

In Revelation 4:8, the Cherubim say "Holy, Holy, Holy, Lord God Almighty, which was, and is, and is to come." The very fact that the Cherubim can do this without any need of rest is not surprising. Since angels are immortal, they need no rest. Now, this does not mean that they cannot rest, but that they need it not. The angels can rest and relax as witnessed by their appearance to Abraham and Lot. (See Genesis 18–19.)

Angels Can Eat Food

Whether angels can truly eat food has been extremely debated throughout the years. Nevertheless, the Scriptures do establish that the angels can eat food of a heavenly nature and food of an earthly nature.

When Abraham visited with the Lord and two angels, the two angels who accompanied the Lord ate physical food. The Lord and the two angels ate bread, parts of a calf, butter, and they drank milk. (See Genesis 18:8.) Only beings that have some type of embodiment can eat food. Disembodied spirits have appetites as witnessed by the fact that demons have a seat of emotions—souls. Yet disembodied spirits, as seen by demons, need a body to fulfill and manifest them. (See Matthew 12:43–45; 8:29; Acts 8:7.) This above all is the purpose for demons to possess a body. They can only do this by inhabiting bodies.

One reason Abraham did not allow Lazarus to dip his finger into water and drip drops of water into the rich man's mouth was because a disembodied spirit can neither eat food nor drink water. (See Luke 16:23–26.)

Remember Genesis 19:1–26 where Lot prepared unleavened cakes for the same two angels who appeared to Abraham with the Lord God. The angels ate these unleavened cakes.

Even in heaven angels are seen to eat food. In Psalm 78:25, the psalmist declared that the manna that fell from the heavens was angels' food. It was the very food that the Israelites in the wilderness were given to eat.

According to Numbers 11, manna in its physical form is like a grain (fruit) of corianders like that of the parsley family, and its color was the color of crystal. The Israelites not only ground it in mills, beat it in mortars, boiled it in pots, but made it up into cakes to be baked. In sweetness, its taste was that of a sweet cake made with oil.

The very fact that God would employ the angels to drop their manna upon the ground so that the Israelites could eat it has reference to the fact that the Israelites were eating a food that is far above any food that can be found on the earth. Its excellence is far above that found on the earth.

According to Matthew 4:11, the angels ministered to Christ in the sense that they prepared and supervised a banquet for Christ with Christ partaking of heavenly drink and food to regain His strength. With the angels eating heavenly food and on occasions physical food, do they acquire waste as humans do after eating? The very appearance of waste and waste by-products from humans eating is not originally how God intended it to be. Waste and waste by-products are a result of sin and rebellion against God. Since the angels of God have never rebelled against Him nor sinned, they do not produce waste and waste by-products when they eat. The angels eat not for strength or to sustain existence but purely for the enjoyment of eating. They also never gain weight because of their eating either. This is also true for fallen angels. Even with certain fallen angels leaving their spiritual realm causing their bodies to become physical, there was no sign of waste and waste by-products.

Apparently, the spiritual bodies of the angels completely absorb the food that they eat whether spiritual or physical. Due to this, no waste or waste by-products are produced. This is the case whether or not their bodies are transformed into physical bodies.

Both Enoch and Elijah who have retained their own natural bodies in heaven do not produce any waste or waste by-products at all. This is done by God reserving their natural bodies without any need for food.

In the pre-fall atmosphere of humanity, Adam and Eve were like the angels in that they could eat for the enjoyment of what had been prepared for them without any waste, waste by-products, and worry of what food was doing to their bodies.

According to Luke 22:30, Christ declared that the apostles in their resurrected state would eat and drink at His table in His kingdom. With the saints in the resurrection being like the angels, then the fact that the angels can eat and drink is affirmed. The saints in their resurrected state will eat for the enjoyment of eating as the angels can do today.

Further evidence conveys that angels have been known to eat food. In the book entitled *Joseph and Aseneth*, the angels eat food. (See Chapter 16, verses 14–15.) In Scripture, angels are seen to be able to eat and even cook if it becomes necessary. (See 1 Kings 19:5–7.)

Angels Can Speak Languages

In Corinthians 13:1, Paul makes a fascinating statement. He declared that he spoke with the languages of angels and languages of men. Of course, this has reference to the manifestation of speaking with tongues that are unknown to the speaker. The speaker has not learned these tongues. Nevertheless, Paul understands that angels can speak and have their own languages.

In 1 Corinthians 13:1 it is seen that angels have their own languages by which they can talk with each other. (See Daniel 10:1–12:13; Zechariah 1:9–11.) Also, the idea expressed is that each order of angels has its own language separate from the other orders, and each order within has its own dialect.

The angelic languages can be used in an audible sense or in an inaudible sense. The languages used in the audible sense express that these languages are spoken with audible words. On the other hand, the languages used in the inaudible sense express that these languages are spoken in thoughts rather than words. In this case, the languages of angels are inaudibly spoken as thoughts. The languages are communicated through thoughts to the recipients' minds.

Such occurrences for Abraham and Lot prove the ability of the angels to speak audibly, (Genesis 18–19) while other instances, as with Daniel, show the angels' ability to speak inaudibly (Daniel 7–12). Of course, in these instances the languages are human. Yet, they show that angels can speak audibly with spoken words or inaudibly with thoughts. The angels possess the knowledge and the means to speak and write all languages of the past and future of the human race. Angels also have the ability to communicate with animals, and the animals back to angels.

According to Jewish tradition, Adam, before his rebellion, could well communicate with all animals upon the earth, and they with him. According to the Babylonian Talmud, the angels know Hebrew.[23] To the Jews, this was very remarkable.

Often, both the Old and New Testaments recount how angels appeared to humans and how they communicated with them. In all of these instances, the angels used human languages to communicate with humans.

However, angels occasionally used their own languages to communicate with other angels or humans whether audibly or inaudibly. (See Job 1:6; 2:1.) In Job 1:6 and 2:1, angels appeared along with Satan before the Lord God and communicated with each other. Satan spoke to the Lord in an angelic language, not in a human language. Since Satan comes from the order of Cherubim, he has his own language and dialect. But the language that Satan was using was not the language of the Cherubim. It was the universal angelic language that all persons and animals in heaven know. Even the saints in heaven know this language.

In 1 Kings 22:19–23, the host of heaven appeared unto the Lord. The Lord spoke in the universal angelic language to the host of heaven and all other beings there. It was this universal angelic language that was the universal language of creation. It was the only language that Adam knew and the only language that all the humans knew before the tower of Babel. (See Genesis 10–11.) It was in this language that God spoke to Adam and Eve in the Garden of Eden. (See Genesis 3:9.) It was in this language that Adam gave the names of the animals (Genesis 2:20), and it was this language that the animals knew and the serpent used to deceive Eve (Genesis 3:1–24).

With the rebellion instigated by Adam all animals lost their ability to speak in this language. This was due to the part the serpent played in the instigation of the rebellion. All animals were thus punished for the serpent's actions. On occasions God will give back to the animals their ability to speak. This is not the universal language of creation, but a common language of humanity. (See Numbers 22:22–35.)

The Ofannim speak unspeakable words. Ezekiel could not speak or comprehend the words of the Ofannim. (See Ezekiel 3:13.) To a hearer of these angelic languages they are unintelligible and bewildering. This was what Paul meant by unspeakable words in 2 Corinthians 12:4.

In 1 Enoch 14:9–23, Enoch, having a vision of heaven, experienced the tongues of fire being part of the outer court of God's palace. The tongues of fire are angelic languages spoken in such a way that they are unspeakable for man. In 1 Enoch 14:2, Enoch speaks of the tongue of flesh, which consists of the languages of humanity. So, Enoch contrasted the languages of humanity with the languages of angels.

In 1 Corinthians 12:10–28, the speaking with diverse kinds of tongues is one gift of the Holy Spirit. Among these are the languages of the angels. In the Testament of Job 48:3, 49:2, and 50:2, the three daughters of Job spoke in the languages of angels. Turning to Daniel 10:11, the uttered phrase "I am speaking to you," is found. It is also found in the Greek Septuagint. The angel Gabriel is speaking to Daniel. This phrase has some very surprising consequences. The supernatural power of an angel is stressed here in that an angel can by supernatural powers speak several things, orders, and revelations to several persons in several directions at once.

Angels Are a Class

In Hebrews 12:22 the angels are not called a race of angels, but "an innumerable class of angels." Luke 20:34–36 proves that angels are not a race. A race is a class of beings that must propagate themselves to sustain their existence, as with humans. A race depends upon itself reproducing by some type of propagation. This deals with those living, not the dead. Once dead, there is no propagation.

Several passages of Scripture show that angels did not fall as a class of spiritual beings, but only certain individual angels did. (See Isaiah 12:12–14; Ezekiel 28:12–19.) Therefore, the fall of many individual angels did not cause the fall of the class of spiritual beings called angels. The fall only dealt with those angels who rebelled against God. The fall of the angels was an individual fall rather than a collective fall.

All the demons fell. However, their sins were individual like that of the fallen angels. Why? Sin committed before Adam is seen as individual; no one creature of God could sin and commit all other creatures into a state of sin and depravity by that one sin. The sin of each individual creature was seen as separate and individual from all others. None of these creatures could be under the power of another in the sense of original sin as in the case of humanity being under the power of Satan.

Angels Are Eternally Young

In Mark 16:5, Mary Magdalene, Mary the mother of James the less, and Solome saw a young man sitting on the side, clothed in a long white garment, and they became afraid. This young man was an angel. The Greek adjective νεανίσκος (nĕänēskŏs) used concerning angels means that the angels are at all times in the prime and vigor of life. This Greek adjective says that the angels are all at the prime and vigor of life being immortal and never aging. Angels are very old in the sense of origin and creation, but there are no outward signs that they are very old. Their outward appearance continues to be seen as it was at their creation: the picture of youth. This same Greek adjective pictures the angels as having the appearance of persons that are from twenty-four to forty years of age. In the resurrection the saints will have this eternal look of youth. According to ancient sources, the saints will have the appearance of persons that are from twenty-four to forty years of age as well.[24] The saints in the resurrection will be like the angels in more than one respect. In actual age, the angels are many billions of years old, but in ideal age they are very young.

Angels Possess Beauty

In Genesis 19, two angels appeared. Such was the beauty of these two angels that the lust of the Sodomites was great. Only the manifestation of God's power kept the Sodomites from taking these angels and committing homosexual acts with them. (See Genesis 19:5.) What a fascinating statement! The beauty of the godly angels overwhelmed the Sodomites in their sexual lusts for them. The Sodomites were so drawn to the angels in lust that they wanted to reach even a lower low and tempt the very representatives of God's power by desiring to have them in sexual immorality.

The fallen angels who invaded the physical realm to have sexual relations with women also possessed this great beauty. According to the Testament of Rebuen 5:6, women were overwhelmed in their sexual lusts for them. Such was the beauty of the fallen angels that the women could not help but give into the fallen angels' desires and propagate.

Angels Have Five Spiritual Senses

In Genesis 18–19 the angels, when transforming their spiritual bodies into physical bodies, can see, hear, touch, smell, and taste. Even in the spiritual realm angels are able to touch, hear, taste, smell, and see. For example, the angel Gabriel in Daniel 10 fought against the satanic chief angel of the Medo-Persian Empire. He did that only by being able to see, touch, and hold his enemy. The abilities of angels to touch, hear, taste, smell, and see are termed the five spiritual senses. These senses are like the five physical senses that humans have, but the five spiritual senses are so superior to those found in humans that they can work both in the physical realm and the spiritual realm simultaneously. The five physical senses that humans have can only work in the physical realm.

Chapter 7

Angelic Works
Commonly Known

Angels Guide

THE PARTICIPATION OF angels in the redemptive work of Christ is well documented in Scripture. They guide and lead preachers in the redemptive work of Christ. They also guide and lead sinners to saints so that they can be saved. In Genesis 19:1–2 and Hebrews 1:14 there is illustrated the fact that angels are active in the divine work of reconciliation and redemption. In Acts 8:26–27, an angel instructs Philip to leave Samaria and go down to Gaza so that he could preach to one man. Therefore, the angel directed Philip where to preach the Gospel. In Acts 10:3–4, Cornelius, a sinner, was instructed where to find a preacher so he could be saved after hearing the Gospel.

Angels Gave the Law

The reality that angels gave the Law of Moses to men is a debate that has lingered. Some drastically deny that the angels had a part in giving the Jewish nation the Law of Moses. This thought distorts Scripture. Many point to the passages where there is no mention of angels dealing with the giving of the law. (See Exodus 19, 20, and 32–34.) These passages seem to demand that God alone gave the law to the Jewish nation with Moses being the mediator of the law. But other passages of scripture show that the law was given to the Jewish nation through the agency of angels. (See Acts 7:53, Hebrews 2:2.)

In Acts 7:53, Stephen confirms that the disposition of angels gave the law. The Greek noun διαταγὴ (thēätäyē) commonly translated as disposition is best translated "arrangements." This means that the law is God's words that God Himself spoke. The words spoken by God were spoken not in a human language, but in the universal angelic language. Because of this, Moses needed an interpreter of what God said. This is where the angels came in. Through their arrangements, the words spoken by God in one language were heard by Moses in another. The angels arranged the law to be heard by Moses in a human language, which was the Hebrew language. They quoted the words of God not in the universal angelic language, but in a human language.

All the angels present at Mount Sinai were interpreting these words of God in the Hebrew language, but Acts 7:38 states that Moses only heard the voice of one angel in several segments since all the law was not given at once. The other angels, except Michael, were speaking quietly so Moses could not hear them. Yet, they were speaking these words as a chorus singing a melody. The voices of these angels were like a hundred upon a hundred voices being spoken together as a sweet melody. The angels were acting and speaking as God coming in the name and person of God by prophesying.

Josephus states that the Jews learned from God their doctrines and their law by angels.[1] Only one angel was speaking directly to Moses the words interpreted and translated of God. According to Jewish tradition a particular angel was known as the angel of the law. This angel spoke directly to Moses the words of God that constituted the law. This angel was Michael, the guardian angel of Israel. Why was Michael given this privilege? Michael was the chief angel over Israel, the guardian angel over them, and the most important angel during the times of the Old Testament. That God spoke to Moses through an angel, Michael, is often well established and has been well discussed in Jewish schools of Theology.

The idea that the law was given by means of the mediation of the angels is well documented in such documents as Jubilees 1:29 and the Testament of Daniel 6:1.

106

Not only does Stephen state that the angels had a part in giving the law of Moses to the Jewish nation, but Hebrews 2:2 proves the same thing. Hebrews 2:2 settles that the word spoken by the angels was firm. What word? The law of Moses. The singular word does not mean that the angels just spoke one word but that they spoke many words as one subject in unity. That subject was the law of Moses. So, all the words spoken by the angels concerned the giving of the law.

The Book of Hebrews 2:2 proves that the angels spoke the words of the law to Moses in the same manner as found in Acts 7:53 and 7:38. God gave the law by the mediators who were none other than the angels.

Paul, in Galatians 3:19, shows that angels were ordaining the law of Moses. The thought follows that of Acts 7:53. God spoke the words of the law in the universal angelic language. The angels arranged what He said in a human language so that Moses could understand.

Both Hebrews 2:2 and Galatians 3:19 refer to the part of the angels in the giving of the law so that the superiority of the gospel to the law could be emphasized.

Why was the law given?

- Because of sin and transgression (Galatians 3:19).

- So that humanity might know what sin is (Romans 3:20).

- So that sin might increase (Romans 5:20).

- So that a state of desperation might continue upon humanity so they would want to seek a Messiah (Galatians 3:10–12).

- So that all would be under the law and need a Messiah (Romans 8:2–4).

- So that the Messiah could confirm and extend the moral precepts of the law (Matthew 5:27–28, 21–22, 33).

- So that Messiah would bring the Mosaic law to an end (Matthew 15:2; Romans 13:10).

- So that it may govern Israel until the time of Messiah (Matthew 11:11–13).

- So that humanity would appear guilty before God (Romans 3:19–20).

- So that the knowledge of sin might be brought forth to humanity (Romans 3:19–20; 4:15).

- So that humanity would be under bondage (Galatians 4:14–31; 5:1).

- So that it would be a shadow of good things to come (Colossians 2:14–17).

- So that humanity would not be righteous (Galatians 3:21).

- To shut up all men under the bondage of sin so that the promise of salvation by faith in Christ might be given to those who believe (Galatians 3:22).

- So that it would act like a teacher in order to lead one to Christ (Galatians 3:23–24).

Angels Give Instructions

In 2 Kings 1:15, an angel appeared to Elijah and instructed him to go down unto the king and be not afraid of him.

In Revelation 10:9, an angel instructed John to take the little book and eat it. To eat up a book is an expression that signifies that one must be thoroughly acquainted with and understand the contents of the book. In other words, to eat up a book means to learn its whole contents eagerly. In this case, it cannot be taken in a literal sense.

God uses angels in this capacity to help:

- His children
- His eternal plan
- Further His glory and holiness

Angels Give Blessings and Promises

In Genesis 32:24–30, the angel gives to Jacob blessings. From the circumstances that surround Genesis 32:24–30, the blessings given by the angel to Jacob were physical blessings that God had ordained, such as a long life, wealth, children, and whatever else that entailed. But not all blessings given by this angel were physical. Spiritual blessings were given too. The angel gave Jacob the new name of Israel which entailed many spiritual blessings. In Genesis 48:15–16 Jacob, in the blessing of Joseph and his sons, mentions the same angel.

While angels are used by God in the capacity of blessing, their blessing is not their personal blessing but a blessing from God given to humans through angels. Undoubtedly, they give the blessings to humans that God has ordained to be given.

As angels work in giving blessings, they work in giving promises. (See Luke 1:11–13.) In this passage Gabriel appears to Zacharias and gives a promise that Elisabeth will give birth to a son. It cannot be said that the angels give their own promises to humans because the promises that they give are God's.

Angels Foretell the Future

The Book of Daniel is filled with angelic aid in dealing with the future. The angels are employed by God as interpreters and revealers of the future to the Jewish people in particular and all humanity overall. For example, why did Gabriel come to Daniel? (See Daniel 10.) To warn Daniel of what would occur to the Jewish people in the immediate future in relation to the kingdoms of the world (Daniel 11:2–34) and in the far away future of Israel and the whole world (Daniel 11:35–12:13). Nevertheless, this warning by Gabriel to Daniel of what would occur to the Jewish people was conditional given. Why? Every prophecy is based on conditions. Because of this, the Lord through the angels was showing Daniel one possible future that would occur if the Jews continued to rebel against Him. As Daniel 9 so adequately conveys along with other passages the Jewish nation was shown two paths to follow. The first one was a path of obedience while the other one was a path of disobedience. The Jews as a whole chose the path of disobedience.

In Daniel 10:13–14, and other scriptures not cited, the capacity of the angels foretelling the future is well attested. Yet, the capacity of the angels foretelling the future is limited, restricted, and can only be done when God informs the angels of what to say.

Angels Give Revelations

Revelation means what? A revelation is knowledge gained by men without learning it by human means. Other definitions of revelation:

- Something revealed that was not previously known by the one whom it was revealed to.

- The disclosing of facts and truths by another means rather than human.

- The disclosing of a mystery, either in a total sense or in a partial sense. Revealing a mystery in a total sense means that the revelation is one whose secrets no man knows before they are disclosed. Disclosing a mystery in a partial sense is one that has already been revealed to some, but not to the ones that it was given to until it was revealed by God or the angels.

Where do revelations come from? They come from two sources. The first source is God who can show mysteries to His saints by Himself or by His angels; the second source is Satan. Satan can reveal these mysteries himself or through his forces. In Daniel 9:21–23, Gabriel came to Daniel to give him a revelation concerning His people.

Angels Protect

In Genesis 48:16 Jacob praises the protective work of the angel who guarded him throughout his life, keeping him from all suffering and calamities. Psalms reveals that God will give His angels charge over the saints to protect, defend, and guard them against the onslaught of Satan and his forces.

From the Greek Septuagint, Psalm 34:7 reads, "An angel of the Lord will place an army of angels around about those who fear him and will deliver them." Who is the angel of the Lord mentioned? This has been a difficult problem. Many state that the angel of the Lord is Christ, but this cannot be. Why? Christ never appeared as the angel of the Lord. If He had, it would damage the claim of His deity. The particular angel unquestionably made mention by David that will place an army of angels around about those who fear God and that will deliver the saints through the army of angels employed by him can be none other than Michael. One of Michael's tasks has been, and continues to be in special times of great conflict, to order other angels to be used in the defense of God's saints against Satan and his forces.

The situation talked about by David does not usually occur. It only occurs when the opposition of Satan becomes so strong that angels have to be employed by God as an army to defend a person from that onslaught. The use of the *future tense* by the Greek Septuagint shows the thought that the situation only occurs occasionally as directed by God and does not concern the usual guarding, protecting, and defending of the saints by angels.

Angels Can Strengthen in Trials

In Luke 22:43, an angel appeared in the Garden of Gethsemane unto Christ to strengthen Him. The Greek verb ἐνισχύω (ĕnēskhēō) means that the angel imparted unto Christ as man the intrinsic power of God Almighty so that Christ as man could withstand the conflict that He was going through in the Garden of Gethsemane. The Greek noun ἀγωνία (ägōnēä) being used in Luke 22:44 is better translated as "violent struggle." This was what was occurring. The angel came to impart supernatural power to Christ so that He could withstand the onslaught of Satan and all his forces who sought to kill Him before He could die on the Cross and, through means of the Cross, accomplish the defeat of Satan. (See 2 Corinthians 4:4; Colossians 1:13; John 12:31–32.) The death of Christ upon the Cross sealed the doom of Satan.

Psalm 34:7 illustrates that angels can be used to deliver one out of trials while Acts 5:17–29 gives another example of angels being used in this capacity. In Acts 5:17–29 it was a particular angel used by God instead of many angels. Other times many angels may be used to strengthen a saint in his or her trials. The greater the conflict and opposition, the greater number or order of angels must be employed.

Angels Ministering

After Satan's temptation of Christ, angels appeared to Christ to minister to Him, according to Matthew 4:11 and Mark 1:13. In what sense did the angels come to minister to Christ? The Greek verb διακονέω (thēäkōnĕō) denotes that the angels came to supply Him the necessities for life since He had been fasting and had gone through a spiritual conflict with Satan. So, it was the task of the angels to supply Christ with food and drink so that His physical body could again be strengthened. The original sense of this Greek verb is, "To wait on a table." In a wider sense though, it means to supervise the meal. In this sense, the angels were the ones who supplied the drink and food for Christ and supervised what would be given as drink and food for Christ. They also supervised the place where this banquet would be held. Such splendor was manifested after the tempting of Christ by Satan. The triumph of Christ over this temptation was celebrated with a massive banquet for Christ. The angels gave Him drink and food of a heavenly origin that was changed into a physical form. The heavenly drink and food had to have its molecular structure changed from that of a spiritual substance to that of a physical substance so that Christ could partake of them since He was in a physical form.

The omission of this very important fact about angels by Luke and John does not at all deter anyone from believing it. The other Gospels did not concern themselves with it since their focus was different from that of Matthew and Mark. With Matthew and Mark bearing witness of this fact, it became repetitive for the other Gospels to mention it again so they left this fact out understanding that Matthew and Mark had already recanted it.

The ministering of the angels, as seen in Hebrews 1:14 and Psalm 104:4, is not different from what is conveyed in Matthew 4:11. Angels minister to whomever God wants. They minister in the way that God so directs them.

It is a fact. Angels are ministers of God especially during the Dispensation of Grace. Their primary ministry is to assist and guide the saints to conform to the will of God and to obey the commands of God. (See Hebrews 11:4; Luke 1:16; Genesis 21:17–21; Proverbs 17:11; Psalm 103:20; Genesis 22:15; Daniel 3:28.) The angels are always ready and able. They are waiting on God to say, "Go and help My saints." *They are ready to be put into action to help the saints.* Since they are completely obedient to God, they will not and cannot go and work without His providence.

In Hebrews 11:4, the Greek text does not mean that the angels are waiting upon the saints and doing their bidding. No! It has reference to the angels fulfilling their office as ministers of God serving Him and doing His bidding as it relates to the heirs of eternal and unconditional salvation. *A saint has not the authority to order angels.* (See Matthew 26:53; Psalm 91:11–12; 103:20; Hebrews 1:14; Matthew 6:10.)

The ministering of the angels towards the saints may be stopped, revoked, or denied if there appear hindrances in the lives of the saints. In my book on gifts, *Just When Did Spiritual Gifts Cease?*, I gave several hindrances to healings. Several of these same hindrances can be seen here to produce sad results when angels are ministering to the saints. In other words, these hindrances can stop, revoke, or deny the assistance of the angels in accordance to God's will. In essence, sin and disobedience will stop or destroy the work of the angels within a person's life, if repentance does not come.

The conditions and ways of setting in motion or motivating the assistance of the angels in the lives of the saints must be pulled from Abraham, other Patriarchs, and other people of the Bible. Angels mostly assisted the saints when they were obedient, living their lives in accordance to God's will, following God's word, speaking God's word in their mouth, having faith, praying in intercession God's will and not their own, praying and fasting in the midst of tears, and refusing to work, live, and act contrary to God's will. (See Genesis 18–19; 24:1–7; Daniel 2; 9–10; Psalm 1:3; 103:20; 2 Kings 6; Matthew 12:37.) But notice that the angels may not assist the saints as they always want. The angel may not save them from death, tribulations, or some perilous times. Yet, the angels follow a higher agenda. They are following what God wants, not what the saints want. If an angel does not appear to assist us in some situation, and we have no hindrances, then we must recognize that God has a plan greater than we can imagine, and God is using that situation to test us.

Above anything else the angels will move when the very covenant between God and His saint is in need of protecting, fulfilling, enforcing, or securing. Angels are covenant-minded creatures after all. They have a covenant with God too.

Angels Appear in Dreams and Visions

What are dreams and visions? Various definitions give a good understanding of what they are:

- A dream/vision is a state by which one enters the spiritual realm and receives through his mind images, pictures, thoughts, and ideas.

- A dream/vision is a supernatural presentation of certain scenery or circumstances to the mind of a person.

- A dream/vision is an act of perceiving mental images that the mind sees.

The only difference between a dream and a vision is that a dream is done when the person is asleep and a vision occurs when one is conscious.

Both dreams and visions occur in the mind. Those experiences mentioned by Paul in 2 Corinthians 12:1–4 were not visions but translations (or raptures). In a translation a person can be caught up bodily as with Enoch, Elijah, and Philip. (See Genesis 5:24; 2 Kings 2:9–12, and Acts 8:39.) Also, in a translation, the spirit can be caught up without the body. In this case, the spirit departs from the body and the body dies for a short period. God preserves the body during the translation. The spirit of the person is then brought back into the body when all has been shown to that person.

The phrase "visions and revelations of the Lord," in 2 Corinthians 12:1–4 is a general statement about supernatural experiences with Paul only mentioning two events that occurred. These two events were revelations through translations. The visions that he had in mind are those mentioned in these passages of Scripture. (See Acts 9:27; 18:9; 22:18; 23:11.) His desire not to mention the visions but center on the translations is an attempt by Paul to underline the greatness of his supernatural experiences being equal to none. He desired to prove beyond a doubt that he was a man of God and silence his critics.

The three prominent sources of dreams and visions are God, Satan, and the minds of men. Our minds do also generate some types of dreams and visions. Visions are known as daydreaming. The dreams and visions generated by our minds have no connection to the spiritual realm. This third source may also be known as the flesh. It comes from us, our desires, wants, and feelings.

How does one tell when dreams and visions come from God? A dream or a vision from God will achieve some godly purpose. It will bear witness to the Word of God, agreeing with it, being something that exhibits God's eternal plan, and it will always bring one nearer to God in His eternal plan.

There are two types of dreams and visions sent from God:

- One is sent by God with things that are common and familiar to the seer. In this type God works to give it in the realm of the seer's capacity to understand it.

- One is sent by God with things that are not common and familiar to the seer. In this type God works to give it outside the realm of the seer's capacity to understand it. Because of this, the seer needs it to be interpreted.

How does one tell when a dream or vision comes from Satan? Ultimately, the dream or vision will achieve some ungodly purpose. It will degrade, confuse, and contradict the Word of God. It also will exhibit Satan's plan, and try to drag a person farther away from God instead of bringing him nearer to God in His eternal plan. Indeed, a dream or vision from Satan is connected to the old life before a person becomes a Christian.

Dreams and visions contain mental images. A mental image is an image seen in a dream or vision that is produced either by the mind apart from God or Satan or through the mind by the influence of God or Satan. It is carried on in the mind to conform to the real image of someone or something. This mental image is an exact likeness and resemblance of the things, persons, and places that they represent, whether real or symbolic.

A very good example of mental images being used in a dream or vision is found in Daniel 7:10–14. It must be known that every angel presented in this vision is real but not the saints. Many Old Testament saints, all the church, all the 144,000 Jews, and all the saints between the Rapture and the end of the Tribulation did not exist at the time of the vision. Therefore, Daniel beheld mental images of people who were represented as God's saints that did not yet exist.

Angels Witness the Repentance of Sinners

It is a known fact that angels behold sinners repenting. This is seen in Luke 15:4–10. They see sinners becoming saints by repentance and accepting

Christ as their Savior. When they behold this, there is much rejoicing done by the angels. Since every day humans are accepting Christ as their Savior, then there is much rejoicing in heaven by the angels every day.

New birth means what? It has a reference to a complete and utter change of ownership from Satan to God. (See Romans 6:15–23.) Then, it is also seen as a new creation of a person by the Word of God, the blood of Christ, the baptism into Christ, and the Spirit of God operating upon and changing that person completely when he repents and accepts Christ. (See Revelation 1:5; Romans 3:24–25; 5:9; 1 John 1:7; Ephesians 2:8; Hebrews 9:22; Titus 3:5.) When this happens, the person experiences the process of being renewed in holiness by grace. Therefore, a state of grace and holiness is found in his life.

Angels Carry Out Miracles

The varieties of miracles that angels do for God are countless in number. On this account, it is impossible to describe or mention all of them unless God Himself gives the list. (See John 5:4; Genesis 19:11; Judges 6:19–24; 2 Kings 19:35; Acts 12:23; Revelation 6–19; Exodus 4:3.)

Angels Bring Encouragement and Comfort

In Matthew 28, there is a gloomy sight at first. Mary Magdalene and Mary, the mother of James the Less, are coming in anguish to the sepulcher and they are full of despair to the sepulcher. As they came, something happened. An angel caused a great earthquake as he descended from heaven. What was the task of the angel? Not only to roll back the stone and sit upon it, but to tell Mary Magdalene and the other Mary these eight words of encouragement: "He is not here: for He is risen."

It is quite interesting that a woman was the first human to preach the resurrection of Christ. The very first being to preach this message, however, was an angel preaching encouragement and comfort.

Angels Blow Trumpets

In Revelation 8:1–11:19, angels will use the blowing of the seven trumpets to signal the commencement of the seven judgments upon the earth.

The very truth that in heaven there are whole choirs and orchestras praising the Lord God with songs is well proved. (See Revelation

8:1–11:19.) This means of praising the Lord God is described to the reader by David in Psalm 150:1–6. In the midst of praising the Lord God with songs, it is recognized that musical instruments are a means by which anyone can praise Him. Such praise continues in heaven now that songs and music are forever echoing throughout the universe as a monument and memorial to God's righteousness, long-suffering, justice, mercy, and grace.

John beheld in a vision in Revelation 5:11–12 a substantial and gigantic heavenly chorus of countless millions praising the Lamb through magnificent music. Many in this chorus seen by John were angels.

Many in the Scriptures have been involved in singing and praising the Lord God: Moses (Exodus 15:1), Miriam (Exodus 15:20–21), many singing to the Lord (Exodus 32:18), Deborah and Barak (Judges 5:1–5), David (2 Samuel 22:50; Psalms), thousands at the temple (2 Chronicles 5:12), thousands preceded the ark of the covenant (1 Chronicles 15:27–28), and others.

Angels Are Interpreters

In the Book of Daniel, Daniel is seen as helpless in interpreting the vision of Daniel 8. Such helplessness is found in Daniel's capacity to understand the vision of Daniel 8 that he, without the help of Gabriel, could not understand the revelation given to him about the conditional future of the Jewish people. In Daniel 8, it was the purpose of Gabriel to come forth and give Daniel the interpretation of what is portrayed in the vision. When angels come as interpreters of dreams and visions given by God, their purpose is to give the interpretation to the saint of God so that the saint will understand what is meant.

This shows that angels have supernatural knowledge, but are not omniscient. What is meant here is that the angels are more knowledgeable than humanity, especially as it relates to spiritual things and the spiritual realm.

By being interpreters of dreams and visions, the angels interpret God's will to men. However, angels can interpret the will of God to men without having to appear in dreams and visions. Angels have appeared in absolute flesh and interpreted the will of God to men. (See Daniel 3:24b–35; Genesis 18:2–33; 19:1–26; 32:24–30; Judges 6:11–22, and Judges 13:1–23.) Even today angels are interpreting God's will to men by means of appearing in absolute, complete, tangible, and visible flesh. (See Hebrews 13:2.)

Angels Find Those Whom God Wills

With angels being spiritual beings, it is not surprising that they can physically find those whom God wills them to. A very good example of this is found in the incident of Hagar when Hagar fled from the face of Sarah into the wilderness. She thought that God could not find her out there, but God proved her wrong. An angel found her there in the most remote place one could imagine. What does this show? That no matter how far one runs, God will find you. In Genesis 16:7–13, an angel found Hagar under the direct will of God and as the direct representative of God.

There are many passages of Scripture that attest that angels can find those whom God wants them to find. (See Genesis 32:24–30; Luke 1:13; Daniel 7:15–16; 8:15–16; 9:21–23; 10:1–12:13; Isaiah 6:1–7; Acts 12:23.) In Revelation 12:7–9 and Daniel 10:12–21, it is seen that this ability transcends humanity. The angels of God can find those satanic angels and demons that are in an ongoing conflict with them and engage in furious battles that transcend any war or battle fought upon the earth. Satanic angels and demons also have the ability to find people and God's angels.

Angels Cast Out the Wicked

In Exodus 33:2, the great power of angels is seen. An angel, Michael, was sent by God to cast the wicked out of the Promised Land by violent force. Michael was and still is the guardian angel of the Jewish nation. It was his duty to cast out of the Promised Land the wicked by judgments so that the Jewish people could inhabit it.

The Greek Septuagint demands that this was accomplished by an angel, not God.

Angels Pre-Warn God's Saints

In Matthew 2:11–19, the angel Gabriel appears to Joseph in a dream to pre-warn him that Herod wants to find Jesus and kill Him. This example is very powerful. It shows that angels can be used by God to warn saints of impending traps of Satan and show saints how to avoid them. When a saint falls into a trap of Satan, it is the saint's fault and never God's fault.

God will always warn His saints of an impending trap. The problem is the fact that many times the saint ignores the warning of God. The saint then becomes entangled in a trap of Satan that God never wanted him to be in from the beginning. It is the saint's stupidity, stubbornness, and unwillingness to be submissive to the direct will of God, the supernatural manifestation of God's power, and to God's moving in the spiritual realm. If the saint will become submissive to God's direct will, the supernatural manifestation of His power, and to His moving in the spiritual realm permanently, he will never find himself in a trap of Satan. We should never allow ourselves to be in a situation that gives Satan the opportunity to tempt us.

Angels Declare God's Word

In Luke 1:26–27, the angel Gabriel declares the Word of God to Mary as it relates to the birth of the Messiah. Mary was to be the mother of the Messiah, and Gabriel was commanded to give this word to Mary.

There are many passages that show that angels can declare God's word. (See Genesis 16:7–13; 32:24–30; Luke 1:13; Daniel 9:21–23.) By this, angels are seen as bearers of God's words, whether they are as orders, commands, interpretations, judgments, instructions, answers to prayer, comfort, encouragement, rebuke, revelations, warnings, tidings, or strong requests.

Angels Are Intercessors

From the Book of Daniel many truths about angels are known. One truth that many overlook is the fact that God in certain situations employs angels as intercessors. An intercessor means what? One who intercedes for someone or for something; one who stands in the gap for something or for someone. The prayer that Daniel prays in Daniel 9:4–19 is in fact an intercessory prayer, with Daniel being the intercessor for himself and the Jewish people in Gentile captivity.

The intercessors pester God repeatedly with prayer until God does something. God may punish; He may move; or He may manifest His power. The very idea of pestering God repeatedly by prayer until He moves has its origin in Old Testament times. Abraham and the other intercessors of the Old Testament pestered God repeatedly.

An intercessor is also known as a "gap-stander." A person that intercedes for something or for someone stands in the gap between that one and another. Indeed, Daniel was a "gap-stander" since he constantly stood in the gap between the Jewish people and God. Christ as man is the "Gap-stander" for He stands between God and man. (See 1 Timothy 2:15.)

In Matthew 18:10, it is known that the angels who rule over individuals behold the face of the Lord as intercessors interceding for the one over whom God has given them charge. They become gap-standers and pesterers of God by prayer to receive some very important answers from the Lord for those whom they rule over as guardians. For example, in Revelation 1:20 and Revelation 2–3, angels being employed by God as intercessors for seven churches are seen.

In Pseudo-Philo 15:5, the writer notes that God employs angels as intercessors for people. Further, this truth is illustrated in Joseph and Aseneth 15:7–8, Tobit 12:12, 12:15, 2 Baruch 6:7, 1 Enoch 9:10, 15:2, 40:9, 47:2, 99:3, Testament of Levi 5:6, and Testament of Dan 6:1–2.

CHAPTER 8

Angelic Works Less Known

Angels Guard and Rule

ONE PRINCIPAL ACT of God's angels is that they guard and rule over various things for God. Only some of these things are examined in Scripture.

In Genesis 3:24–25, God uses two Cherubim to guard the gate of Eden to intimate that only when humanity had become purified and perfected could they enter paradise. So, the purpose of the Cherubim was to guard the entrance of the Garden of Eden.

In Revelation 21:12, twelve angels are destined to guard the twelve gates of New Jerusalem when it comes down from heaven. When New Jerusalem comes down, all rebels will have already been thrown into the Lake of Fire. (See Revelation 20:11–15.) Then why have guards?

- ◆ To allow all earthly people who are in the Lamb's Book of Life that survived the Millennial kingdom to enter New Jerusalem.

- ◆ To keep all earthly people from dwelling permanently in New Jerusalem.

- ◆ It is clear, from Revelation 21:24–27, that earthly people who lived during the Millennium and those who are born afterward, can on occasion traffic and do business with the rulers and kings of New Jerusalem, bringing their glory and honor to God. They shall be able to survive such a long time because they shall be able to eat of the Trees of Life.

In Revelation 1:20 angels are guardians of seven churches. This proves that over every church an invisible ruler is the real ruler and guardian. These angels are chief angels. The reality that the seven individuals spoken about in Revelation 1:20 and Revelation 2 and 3 are angels and not pastors is clearly understood. Angels are considered the spiritual authority over churches and their representatives. The following points will prove this:

- The clear language of John, in the Greek language, gives the untold sense that angels are meant rather than men of any kind.

- The symbolism used in Revelation 1:20 and Revelation 2 and 3 unequivocally proves that angels are meant rather than pastors. Revelation 1:20 reads, "The seven stars are the angels of the seven churches, and the seven candlesticks are the seven churches." This contrast between heavenly and earthly fires means a great deal. The stars are seen shining steadily by their own inherent and immortal light while the lamps are seen flickering off and on with uncertainty in their future, requiring to be fed with fuel. From this, the heavenly is seen as a representative of the earthly and is seen to be responsible for the earthly to a degree absolutely unsuited to any human pastor. Then, by this contrast, pastors are not the individuals meant here.

- The constant use of the noun *angel*, in the Book of Revelation, never refers to pastors, but always to angels.

- The introduction of the phrase "angels of the waters" without any explanation in Revelation 16:5 means that John used the noun *angel* throughout the Book of Revelation in only one sense. This sense is that of spiritual beings.

- The very expression of Christ in Matthew 18:10 proves that angels are stationed as guardians over various things, one being individuals. This shows that if angels are allotted to persons, then there is nothing at all strange with the notion that they are allotted to individual churches.

- The words spoken of in the house of Mary, the mother of John, in Acts 12:15 prove the belief that angels are allotted to persons and various other things including churches.

- In all apocalyptic writings the noun *angel* is always used in describing real angels.

- In the early church the exaltation of pastors in this fashion was forbidden. Pastors were always regarded as a member of the church or just part of the community and never exalted above it.

- The early church knew no other interpretation than angels in Revelation 1:20, and Revelation 2–3. The reason is that by believing that angels guard churches, they believed that the Holy Spirit caused their fears to be lessened and would reveal to them that they have supernatural protection through the angels who were the supernatural patrons of the churches.

- The early church accepted the truth that angels were guarding churches by the declaration in the book entitled *The Ascension of Isaiah*. This book promotes that Christianity has one chief guardian angel over it. This angel is considered the angel of the Christian Church. He is Gabriel and is the most important angel in New Testament times.

- The article in front of the nouns *angel* and *angels* in Revelation 1:20 and 2–3 not only recognizes these individuals as angels, but also proves it.

- In Revelation 2:18, the angel of the church in Thyatira is shown to be separate from those servants whom Jezebel taught nothing but deceptions and lies. Because of that, the term *servants* has reference to humans while *angel* has reference just to that—an angel.

- That Christ did not address the seven letters to seven individuals is definitely meant by the *dative case* of the article. The *dative case* of the article does not mean "to" in the seven letters as commonly done by translators, but "for the sake of." So, what is meant is, "For the sake of…write…" The reason the letters were written by John was to answer the petition and intercession of the seven angels for the churches, while the letters were being addressed to the churches themselves.

- Since each angel was the spiritual ruler of his own church, then it was for their sakes that Christ answered their petition concerning the churches.

- Angels over churches are petitioning God on the behalf of their churches.

- The very structure of the Book of Revelation, and how John wrote it proves that angels are intended and not any kind of men.

- The use of the term *stars* shows that whomever it denotes has a heavenly origin rather than an earthly origin. Angels are called stars. (See Job 38:7; Psalm 148:2.)

- The use of the term *candlesticks* as emblems of the churches shows that the churches in their earthly whole are meant, including their pastors.

- The separation of the stars and the candlesticks in the passages shows that each is not of the same origin or the same thing.

- There is remarkable harmony between this fact and other parts of Scripture.

- It lies against common sense to describe and try to prove that the individuals over the seven churches are pastors rather than angels.

In Revelation 9:1 and 20:1–3, the very notion that the holy angels of God are guarding and ruling over the underworld is well established. The angels who guard and rule over the underworld are chief angels.

In Revelation 9:1, it is reported that a star fell from heaven unto the earth and to him was given the key of the bottomless pit. *The star* is a name given to angels. That the star is a person is well illustrated by the personal pronouns "him" and "he." That the person is an angel is well proven by the fact that angels are called "stars" more than once in Scripture. (See Job 38:7; Revelation 12:3–4.) The angel, who is unfallen, is given a literal key to the bottomless pit. The one who gave him the key is none other than Christ since Christ has authority and power over the entire underworld. (See Matthew 8:29; Luke 8:31; Revelation 1:18.) The noun *key* is taken figuratively as meaning "Authority and power to achieve something, or over something." In Matthew 16:19, the noun *key* is used to symbolize the authority and power to achieve something. But in Revelation 9:1 the noun *key* is seen as a literal key. This literal key will be used in the future to unlock the bottomless pit by a particular angel to loose countless millions of demons. In Revelation 20:1–3 the noun *key* is seen also as a literal key. This literal key will be used again in the future by the same particular angel mentioned in Revelation 9:1. This time the literal key will open the bottomless pit so that Satan can be bound with a chain and thrown into the bottomless pit. Also, countless angels of God will throw all the forces of Satan which are loosed into the bottomless pit. (See Isaiah 24:21–22.)

The very truth that Christ will give this angel a literal key to the bottomless pit to open it shows that the bottomless pit is a literal place. Consequently, God evidently has other angels guarding and ruling over the entire underworld. These angels, by God's permission, can enter the prisons there at will without any harm upon their persons.

Before Christ the angels brought the redeemed saints to paradise to reside until the day of Christ when He would release them from that prison. Now, since Christ conquered death and Sheol-Hades, this prison is empty. All the saints now ascend to heaven along with the angels who are their guardians on the earth. The angels of God take the righteous souls to heaven; fallen angels in return take the souls of the unjust to the torment compartment of Sheol-Hades. (See Luke 16:19–31; Revelation 20:13–14.) The wicked are the property of evil. As such, evil collects them and takes them to the underworld.

To conclude, God has many millions of His angels guarding and ruling over the entire underworld. If they were not there, then Satan would have almost a free hand in the underworld. With such freedom, Satan could well loose the angels that are prisoners in Tartarus, all the wicked dead from their prison, all the evil spirits who are prisoners in the bottomless pit or all three prisons simultaneously. It is also understandable that the angels of God who guard and rule over the entire underworld have the keys to unlock and lock certain prisons at will, though not all. These keys can only be given by Christ.

In Deuteronomy 32:8, Daniel 12:1, 10:13–21 and Exodus 23:20, the idea of chief angels ruling over nations is well attested. Exodus 23:20 brings to light that the chief angel over Israel, Michael, was guarding and ruling over Israel in the wilderness.

When a chief angel over a nation or kingdom is overthrown, the nation or kingdom falls. A nation or kingdom cannot be defeated without the chief angel over it being defeated first. These chief angels are the power holding up the nations or kingdoms through God's permission.

Furthermore, the more sinful a nation becomes the more evil angels take positions of power within that nation. And the more evil angels in these positions, the more chance that nation has to be ruled over by a satanic chief angel. But the more righteous a nation becomes the more godly angels take positions of power within that nation, and the more godly angels in these positions the more chance that nation has to be ruled over by a godly chief angel. The same must also be said concerning the chief angel over a nation. If a chief angel over a nation is evil, the dominate force within that nation will be evil. On the other hand, if a chief angel over a nation is good, then the dominate force within that nation will be good. In essence, who rules over a nation determines just who will be most of the rulership in that nation.

Occasionally, the defeat of a chief angel over a nation or kingdom only has a spiritual effect. In these occasions, no physical effect such as a physical enemy defeating a nation or kingdom will be seen. Only the spiritual life of a nation or kingdom is changed either for better or for worse.

In the *Midrash Rabbah* this is seen.[1] It purports that chief angels were and are the guardian angels over the nations or kingdoms. When a chief angel over a nation or kingdom falls so does it in one way or another. The authors of the *Midrash Rabbah* saw that Genesis 28:12 meant not only that Jacob saw the angels of God ascending and descending on a stairway, but that this meant that angels were rising and falling as their nations and kingdoms were. (See Isaiah 24:21–22; Daniel 8 and 10.)

In Matthew 18:10, the doctrine that each person has at least one angel over him or her is well proven. Many persons have more than one angel who works in this capacity. Therefore, there is no definite number of angels employed by God to guard and rule over each individual. These angels are chief angels.

The idea expressed by "always" in Matthew 18:10 affords proof to the fact that the angel employed in this capacity is not withdrawn by God. On the other hand, at the time of accountability, the guarding and ruling position of the angel over a person is greatly weakened. This continues until that person accepts Christ and is saved by grace through faith.

In Pseudo-Philo 11:12, 15:5, 59:4, the Book of Jubilees 25:17, Testament of Dan 5:4, Testament of Joseph 6:7, Testament of Benjamin 6:1, the Apocalypse of Abraham 10, and the Books of Adam and Eve 21, angels being understood to be guardians is well seen to be the belief of antiquity.

In Revelation 7:2–8, 14:18, 16:5, and 10:1–11, it is definitely stated that angels guard and rule over the elements of the world. Satan's angels also have this ability. From these same verses, it is learned that God's angels guard and rule over those parts of the physical realm that are found in God's kingdom. Though this is quite true, God's angels maintain and run the entire realm for Him. Therefore, the continued running of the physical realm has been given over to God's angels. It is through them that the physical realm runs and keeps its continued operation going. For example, the rising and setting of the sun are due to God's angels. How? They set in motion the movement and working of all the planets, galaxies, solar systems, and whatever else. Then, the maintenance of the universe, including the spiritual and physical realms, is under the directions of His angels. Yet, they do not sustain or preserve the existence of the universe. They only maintain and run it for God.

Angels also have power over directions according to Revelation 7:2. In the Book of Jubilees 2:2, angels are recognized as being able to control the physical realm. The Seraphim guard and rule over very great groups of galaxies. The Cherubim guard and rule over no less than one galaxy while the Ofannim guard and rule over not less than one solar system.

Angels and Their Station

Where are angels stationed? Angels employed by God in this manner do not have to station themselves by these things. The power of angels is extensive. For this reason, the angel does not have to be literally over a thing or by a thing to do this work.

However, chief angels occasionally do leave their station in the heavenlies where they rule and literally come forth to the place on the earth over which God has given them rule. Also, on occasion other angels are not stationed in the heavenlies to rule, but are stationed on earth to accomplish this task. The only angels who set up their rulership in the heavenlies are the chief angels. Any other angels used by God in this particular manner must come down to the earth to do it.

Furthermore, the Seraphim, Cherubim, Ofannim, and certain chief angels do this work not upon the earth. Since they rule over vast areas of God's kingdom, they do not have to be literally by everything that they guard and rule.

As it relates to kingdoms, nations, states, provinces, cities, towns, districts, doors, and whatever else upon the earth, chief angels are the ones who guard and rule them. Yet, they use common angels as their representatives to help fulfill their mission. As seen, mostly in the Scriptures the work of guarding and ruling over various things is restricted to the chief angels. Yet, all angels have this ability, and almost all angels do work somehow in this manner.

Why does God have angels employed in this capacity? Since the rebellion of Satan, there has been an ongoing "tug-of-war" between God and Satan. There have been many wars and battles between God and Satan since the beginning of the rebellion. Both universal and local battles have been fought. When it comes to a universal war and battle, Satan has never had success, but when it comes to local wars and battles, Satan does have success.

In the tug-of-war that is ongoing between God and Satan, there are consecutive battles and wars being fought for position, power, spoils, and territories in the second heaven, the first heaven, and on the earth. The kingdom of God and the kingdom of Satan both have dominion over the earth, fighting each other for more areas of control. As seen, both God and Satan have an organized kingdom. There is such importance in occupying areas that many wars and battles fought between God and Satan are only over one home, one block of area, one yard of area, or even one foot. Such extensive battles and wars are fought with fury just over a small piece of area that it is almost impossible for mere humans to comprehend it.

In a spiritual perspective, it is clearly seen. Since the rebellion of Satan and his forces, the main desire of Satan has been to rule over all creation. Therefore, the reason that battles and wars are found in fury is because Satan will never be satisfied until he controls all creation and puts God under his feet. With God not standing for this, He counterattacks with great force against the ambitions of Satan. While there are powerful wars and battles being fought, the winner of creation has already been determined. All creation will become God's without any bit of rebellion found in it. (See Revelation 20:7–9.) Above everything else, this is what God's being "all in all" means. (See 1 Corinthians 15:28.) God will have absolute rule over all creation without any bit of rebellion. So, the kingdom of God contrasting the millennial kingdom will constitute all the area of creation again.

The rebellion of Satan split the original creation into two kingdoms. This remains until God is all in all.

Does this belief about an ongoing tug-of-war between God and Satan constitute heathen dualism? What is heathen dualism? It is the belief in two eternal and equal forces that are impersonal, having no personality, that war eternally over control of the universe.

Six points disprove that this is heathen dualism:

- In the conflict between God and Satan, only God is eternal while Satan is created.

- God and Satan are personal.

- The conflict has not been on going eternally. It has an end. (See Revelation 20:7–10.)

- God has already determined Himself the winner in this war.

- God and Satan are not equal in power.

- This war is allowed by God Himself under His sovereignty and under His control to stop. The time that God has decided to end it is after the Millennium. (See Revelation 20:7–10.)

Creation/God All in All

The term *creation* or *all creation* usually means all the area and materials of the universe. The materials are God's heaven, planets, stars, galaxies, solar systems, and whatever other inanimate objects there are. The term can encompass all things God created, everything that God created except all free moral agents, or all except some that He created. The context will determine what is meant.

When the term *creation* or *all creation* is used about God having absolute rule over all creation without any bit of rebellion, the term means all the area and materials created in each realm and all free moral agents that God created, except rebels. There will always be rebels against God. Nevertheless, there is a time coming when these rebels will all be imprisoned in the Lake of Fire so that all the area, materials, and other free moral agents created in the universe will be His without any rebellion against His absolute rule. At this time, the rebels will no longer be considered a part of creation.

Acts 3:21, Romans 5:18, and Colossians 1:20 mean that all who will conform to God's eternal plan will be reconciled, and all creation will be restored to the original perfect state after God has complete rule over it. The restoration requires there to be a Lake of Fire so that it can be accomplished.

The term *all things* or *all created things* means the same thing as the term *creation* or *all creation*.

According to the scriptures, angels were the first ones to rule over all created things. The *all things* or *all created things* that the angels ruled over have reference to all the area and the materials of the universe and any other free moral agents created. It does not include the angels who were the rulers over these things.

Man was the second to rule over all things. That included all the area and the materials of the universe and any other free moral agents created that he ruled over in the universe. The saints will inherit and rule over the same things as did man before the fall. The saints will not rule over any rebel. Why? All rebels are destined to be in the Lake of Fire.

Greek grammar demands that *all in all* has reference to God's absolute and supreme rule being restored without any bit of rebellion. Therefore, God will again completely rule over all created things. This definitely means that the kingdom of God will include all created things and again be in union with all things without any hint of rebellion.

On this ground, God will become all in all over everything, just as before the rebellion of Satan. (See 1 Corinthians 15:24–28; Ephesians 1:10.) What does this mean? That His kingdom will encompass all created things, which signifies the absolute rule of God is again reinstituted because of no rebellion. Christ as the exalted man will rid the earth of all rebels. (See 1 Corinthians 15:24–28.) This is the only way for the kingdom of God to again become all things.

Christ and His Millennial Reign

The Millennium and the millennial reign of Christ as man will only last a thousand years, but the millennial kingdom and His eternal reign as God when the Millennium ends will continue forever. They will never cease since both will continue forever. (See Isaiah 9:6–7; Daniel 2:44–45; 7:13–14; Revelation 22:5.) Therefore, the Millennial kingdom after the end of the Millennium will still exist, but as part of the kingdom of God and not separate from it. After the Millennium, when the heavens and the earth are restored into perfection and sinlessness, the Millennial kingdom will be submerged into the kingdom of God forever. At that time, Christ as God will share in its rule like the rest of the kingdom of God with the other members of the Godhead. (See John 18: 28–37; 1 Corinthians 15:24–28; Revelation 19:11–20:10.) Therefore, its independence from the kingdom of God will end.

The mediatorial office of Christ between God and man will be brought to an end as well. At this time, Christ will stop reigning as man and from that point on will only reign as God. But this does not mean that Christ will give up His humanity. First Corinthians 15:24–28 has reference to Christ's humanity while Luke 1:32–33 has reference to Christ's deity. As a man He will receive a kingdom and as a man He will deliver it up. Nevertheless, a kingdom is pertaining to Christ that will have no end, which He has never been given, and that kingdom is the kingdom of God.

Angels Fight in Real Wars

In the second heaven, there is no peace or silence. In the different zones of space, there is anarchy. Countless wars and battles are raging ceaselessly in its boundaries. The battles and wars that rage are real. Who are the participants? According to Revelation 12:7–9, the main participants in those conflicts are the angels of God and the angels of Satan. So, these groups attack each other with tireless onslaughts trying to tear down each one's stronghold. They use swords, spears, shields, armor, and whatever else is needed to win these struggles. Why are these battles and wars fought? There are several reasons for their fighting. To sum them all up in one statement, the main reason for these conflicts is to further the plans of their masters. What is the plan of Satan? The plan of Satan is to overthrow God and gain rulership over all creation. What, then, is the plan of God? The plan of God is to have a universal kingdom over which He will preside over free moral agents who have been thoroughly tested and purged of all possibilities of rebellion, so that God can show the exceeding riches of His grace toward them in all the ages to come without fear of eternal rebellion.

As seen, angels can engage in real and physical fights with each other. The angels of God also can engage in combat with demons and humans. (See Genesis 32:24–30.)

The angels of God can have conflicts with enemies in all areas, including the first heaven, the second heaven, and the third heaven. The first heaven is the sphere that surrounds the earth. (See Genesis 1:1; Daniel 4:12.) It is also known as the atmosphere. The second heaven is the heaven that comprises the universe apart from God's heaven. (See Genesis 1:1; Nehemiah 9:6; Isaiah 40:12; 45:12.) It is also called the *heavenlies*. The third heaven is God's abode. (See 2 Corinthians 12:1–3; Genesis 1:1; Nehemiah 9:6; Isaiah 40:12; 45:12.)

Both the chief angels of God and those of Satan reside in the heavenlies. It is here that they set up their rulership over the kingdoms, nations, states, provinces, cities, towns, districts, doors, and whatever else on the earth. They occasionally go down to the earth for certain reasons.

It is in the heavenlies where the chief angels of both God and Satan fight furious battles and wars over the areas of the earth. The chief angels of God have as their support the countless common angels. Other higher angels of God can come if it is necessary. The fallen chief angels have to support the countless fallen common angels and other higher fallen angels if it is necessary.

From Daniel 10:13 one of the countless conflicts is seen. The spiritual conflict that is brought to light by Daniel involved Michael and Gabriel's fighting against the satanic chief angel over the Medo-Persian Empire. Why did God want Daniel to write about this conflict? So that humans would recognize several important truths about the spiritual realm and its effect on the physical realm. God wants the following truths to be known from the spiritual conflict described by Daniel:

- Nations, kingdoms, and whatever else on the earth have their visible and invisible rulers.

- As with human rulers, these spiritual rulers may or may not be loyal to God.

- There is a constant warfare taking place in the spiritual realm.

- These disloyal spiritual rulers do all in their power to stop and hinder any advance for the kingdom of God.

- This whole scene shows that there exists a direct link between what is occurring on the earth and what the two conflicting spiritual forces are doing.

- Therefore, whatever occurs on the earth about conflicts has already been decided in the heavenlies through other conflicts. The issue of titanic struggles in the heavenlies determines the course of events in the earth.

- Some nations, kingdoms, and whatever else on the earth have rulers in the heavenlies under satanic appointment and in satanic interest.

- Some nations, kingdoms, and whatever else on the earth have rulers in the heavenlies under God's appointment and in God's interest.

- So strong is the satanic opposition and so often formidable is the satanic coalition that mighty angels of God are required to ally themselves together in mutual and reciprocal assistance.

- This scene throws light upon all human history as a drama of God's providence working in different dispensations through which God, in spite of the most gigantic opposition, is accomplishing on earth His purposes.

◆ This scene opens the eyes of a person to the spiritual realm and the constant struggle between good and evil that is ongoing throughout the universe.

Such furious conflicts are fought in the heavenlies that they last hundreds of years. For example, the battle that concerned Michael and Gabriel's fighting against the satanic chief angel over the Medo-Persian Empire lasted for more than 200 years. (See Daniel 10.) Further, there appear furious conflicts over areas that are not on the earth but places in the heavenlies. All orders of spiritual beings in God's kingdom are involved in these conflicts. Undeniably, in these battles and wars areas are lost and gained by both opposing sides.

There are countless conflicts fought between the angels of God and satanic forces. Yet, no one has ever been killed in them. Why? Angels, whether godly or evil, cannot die. And demons are unable to abandon the spiritual realm since they lack bodies. To die physically, one must have a physical form.

The military strategy in these conflicts is to overwhelm their opponents with brute force so much so that one can capture the place held by them.

In the prayer of Joseph, there is mentioned a battle between angels. Also, in the Apocalypse of Abraham (10:9; 18), there is seen a battle between angels.

Evidently, in the heavenlies, a person must pass through corridors to reach the other side. Gabriel had to pass through a corridor to reach Daniel. The satanic chief angel guarded the corridor that he had to pass through, which represented the dominion of the Medo-Persian Empire. The only way for Gabriel to go through this corridor to a desperate Daniel was through this satanic chief angel who would fight against him.

Angels Can Prophesy

This work of angels is overlooked by many. This will be discussed more in the second book on angels.

St. Augustine, an Early Church Father, understood that angels can prophesy by saying:

But if we pass on to that which follows, the angel altogether speaks as a prophet, and reveals expressly that God is speaking by the angel.[2]

Angels Drive Chariots and Spiritual Horses

Second Kings 2:12, 6:13–17, Zechariah 1:7–15, and 6:1–8 are limited in reference to the fourth order of angels. These passages show that angels can drive chariots and ride on horses. All angelic beings can do this, but the fourth order always does it. These angels are the very scouts and spies of the Most High God.

In Revelation 19:14, the armies are the saints and the angels coming with Christ at His Second Coming. The angels are riding horses like the saints.

Angels Carry Out Judgments

The reality that angels have the very ability to carry out judgments for God is nothing surprising. As long as there is sin, God will move to vindicate His holiness by judgments.

The judgments carried out by angels are divided into three types:

The first type of judgment can be mental sickness and other kinds of sicknesses that come upon the wicked and disobedient saints. (See Daniel 4; Luke 1:11–20; Acts 12:23.) In this type, judgments are only sicknesses. The result may or may not be death. It depends upon the severity of the sin and the will of the person that the judgments are being set upon.

The second type of judgment is oppression, chastisement, and persecution to bring forth the vindication of God's holiness. (See 1 Chronicles 21:12–30; Numbers 22:22–23.) There are many scriptures that prove this. In this type, the angels have a great variety of means to bring forth judgments against the wicked and the disobedient saints. Death may be a result from this type of judgment. The direct purpose is to turn a person from their sins to God. The only reason many wicked persons are still alive is because God can still deal with them up to a certain degree. When this ends, the person's life ends.

The third type of judgment is death and destruction. Death and destruction are the only outcomes. (See Exodus 4:24; Genesis 19:13; 2 Samuel 24:16; Isaiah 37:36.) It must be recognized that since the angels come as God's representatives and are under God's rule, then they only do what God tells them to do. In that, if because of repentance God desires to suspend the judgments, the angels must obey and suspend them even in the midst of accomplishing them. (See Exodus 4:24; 1 Chronicles 21:12–30.)

Angels Receive Souls

This is a wonderful operation that the angels accomplish. When a saint dies, he is carried away by God's angels to paradise. What paradise? The answer is found in the term *Abraham's bosom*. This phrase has reference to a place situated under the surface of the earth as one compartment of the underworld. It was this place where all the righteous souls had to go after death before the resurrection of Christ. In this place, the righteous souls were held captive by Satan and had to be delivered by Christ so that they could enter heaven. (See Ephesians 4:8–11; Luke 16:26–31.) After Christ released them from their prison, they were taken to the abode of God. (See Ephesians 4:8–11.) The only ones that ascended to heaven before Christ's resurrection were Elijah and Enoch who did not physically die. (See Genesis 5:23; Hebrews 11:5; 2 Kings 2:11–12.)

There are two ascensions of Christ. The first one is recorded in John 20:17. It is this time when He proclaimed to all in heaven that His physical death had fulfilled and accomplished atonement for humanity in its fullness on the Cross. The second one is recorded in Acts 1:9–11, where He ascended so that the Holy Spirit could descend.

In Luke 16:19–31, it is known that the angels were involved in carrying the souls of the departed saints to paradise. Yet this has ended. Now, the angels carry the souls of the departed saints to heaven.

Angels Rebuke and Curse

In Judges 2:1–5, it is seen that the angels can rebuke the wicked or the disobedient saints. To rebuke simply means that one is scolding someone in a very sharp manner. It also means to address in sharp and severe disapproval of what one is doing. In rebuking Satan and his forces in the name of Jesus though, it means that one is forcing them back by means of the authority of Christ. (See Matthew 4; John 14:14; Acts 2:21–38.)

As seen in Judges 2:1–5, the rebuke by the angel was done by his coming in the name and person of God by prophesying. A rebuke is so severe an action that an angel can only do this by coming in this manner.

In Judges 5:23, an angel pronounces a curse upon Meroz because it would not come to the aid of the Jewish people in a battle.

Angels Gather the Elect

Between the Second Coming and the beginning of the Millennium, Christ will order the angels to gather the elect from the four winds. (See Matthew 24:31.) Who are *the elect*? The Greek adjective ἐκλεκτός (ĕklĕktōs) connected to Matthew 24:22 and 25:40 gives the answer. According to the use of this Greek adjective, the church or any Gentile is not what is referred to, but what is meant is the Jewish people. The purpose in this is so that the regathering of the Jewish people will be brought to an end. The completion of the regathering of the Jewish people is very important. The Jewish people cannot become an eternal nation under their Messiah unless their regathering is completed. The angels of God will bring forth this completion.

The event spoken of in Matthew 24:31 and Mark 13:27 is also mentioned in Isaiah 11:10–15 where Isaiah prophesies that the Jewish people will be completely regathered from the whole world. Isaiah sees the end of this regathering when all of it will be accomplished. Isaiah declares that the Messiah will do it. But how will He do it? Christ Himself mentions how this will be done. It will be accomplished through the angels of God.

These elect are those Jews who will still be alive after the Battle of Armageddon. Christ calls the elect in Matthew 25:40 "brethren." In other words, the elect are those in whom Christ is physically kin to by blood, coming from the same race, which is the Jewish race.

Matthew 13:41–49 describes the judgment of the nations where the wicked will be separated from the godly. (See Matthew 25:31–46.) The wicked will be thrown into the Lake of Fire while the godly will be allowed entrance into the Millennial kingdom because of this judgment. The angels will have a part in this.

This judgment will concern the nations and how they have treated the Jews from the time of the Rapture to the time of the Second Coming. (See Matthew 25: 31–46.) Joel 3:1–2 reveals that this judgment will be based upon how the nations treated Israel not in the past ages or years, but the time from the Rapture to the Second Coming.

Angels Can Bind Enemies

In Daniel 4:17b, according to the Greek Septuagint, Nebuchadnezzar is warned through a dream of the impending judgment of God upon him. In this judgment, God took away the Babylonian Empire from Nebuchadnezzar for a season, gave it to another person, and caused His angels to smote Nebuchadnezzar with a mental illness among other things. (See Daniel 4:15, 17b, 25, 26, 31b, 31c, 31d, and 32.) This mental illness was zoanthropy. (See Daniel 4:32.) Nebuchadnezzar suffered for nearly seven years with a disease of the mind called zoanthropy. During this time, he actually believed that he was an ox. With this form of mental illness, Nebuchadnezzar was so insane that the angels literally bound him with handcuffs and fetters. He was so insane that the angels had to give him food and water. These handcuffs and fetters were physical and were placed on Nebuchadnezzar so that he would not escape. The angels made them. How? By the power of manipulation over matter. This was not an act of creation but taking what God had already created and changing the matter into handcuffs and fetters.

In Revelation 20:1–3 we read about one event that takes place between the Second Coming and the Millennium involving an angel coming down to bind Satan with a chain and throw him into the bottomless pit. All fallen angels and all demons who are loosed will also be thrown into the bottomless pit by countless angels. (See Isaiah 24:21–22.) By this, they will be bound. Satan is the only one who will literally be bound with a chain. (See Revelation 20:1–3.) The rest are bound in the sense that they will be imprisoned in the bottomless pit. The forces of Satan will be imprisoned and cannot hinder the working of Christ during the Millennium. (See Isaiah 24:21–22.)

The pronoun *they* found in Isaiah 24:21–22, according to the Greek Septuagint, has reference to countless angels throwing all the forces of Satan who are currently loosed into the bottomless pit. In the Book of Jubilees 10:9, the reality that angels have the ability to bind up the enemies of the Lord God is affirmed.

Angels Will Accompany Persons to Earth

At the Second Coming of Christ, angels will accompany God the Father, Christ, and the saints to the earth to take back the earth from Satan,

Antichrist, the False Prophet, the evil forces of Satan, and all human rebels. (See Daniel 7:13–14; Matthew 25:31; 2 Thessalonians 1:7–8.) The angels will be employed as warriors in this capacity along with the saints who come with Christ.

At the Second Coming, God the Father, God the Holy Spirit, the saints, angels, Israel, and all the other forces of good will be at Christ's side. Likewise, on Satan's side there will be Antichrist, fallen angels, demons, and many evil men from many nations.

Angels Manifest the Power of God

Daniel 8:10, according to the Greek Septuagint, is a representation of a scene that will occur in the near future. It represents when the kingdom of Antichrist will be exalted beyond the stars, when the kingdom of Antichrist will be struck to the ground by means of these stars, and when these same stars will trample the kingdom of Antichrist down under foot.

The kingdom of Antichrist will be exalted to a greater level and rank than the stars of heaven in the thinking of Satan, Antichrist himself, and millions of Antichrist's subjects and allies.

The stars of heaven represent the power of God that will be manifested both through the agency of angels and without. Some stars represent angels bringing forth God's power while others just represent God's power being brought forth by another means. Therefore, God can use angels to manifest His power in them. It is a known truth that God will use angels to bring judgments against the kingdom of Antichrist.

Angels Have the Ability to Write

In Daniel 5:5, fingers of a hand appeared visibly writing something upon the wall of Belshazzar's palace. The writing by the fingers of this hand was visible. The fingers of this hand were the fingers of an angel. The letters and message written by the fingers of this angel were heavenly. The writing concerned the judgment of the Most High God upon the Babylonian Empire and the city of Babylon.

Jewish tradition states that the one who appeared here and permitted only his fingers to be seen was not God, but an angel. This occurrence is definitely marked to be a manifestation of an angel rather than God. A manifestation of God would be clearly known to be an appearance of God.

According to Jewish tradition, the ink used was heavenly ink, and it was red. The red ink is a picture of Christ's blood that would be shed for humanity. Some believe that this was a picture of the future of the Babylonian Empire and the city of Babylon. Both would run with blood because of the slaughter that would be initiated against the Babylonians by the Medes and Persians in their conquest of the Babylonian Empire.

Angels Teach

Do angels have the ability to teach? To answer this very perplexing question we must examine the early church's teachings on this subject.

Basil the Great writes:

> And so the apostle, knowing the angels to be set over men as tutors and guardians, calls them to witness.[3]

St. Augustine writes:

> Hear an angel teaching. He was teaching a disciple of Christ, and showing him many wonders in the Revelation of John: and when some wonderful vision had been shown him, he trembled, and fell down at the angel's feet; but that angel, who sought not but the glory of God, said, "See thou do it not; for I am a fellow-servant of thee, and of thy brethren the prophets."[4]

In the Book of Jubilees 3:15 and 12:26, angels are seen to be able to teach and instruct men, whether sinners or saints. In the Testament of Reuben 5:1–3, an angel taught Reuben about the condition of women and to be careful when he deals with them.

The ability of angels to teach sinners and saints is well attested by the Scriptures. It was an angel who taught Cornelius where to go for help on how to be saved. (See Acts 10:1–35.) It was an angel who preached the message of Christ's resurrection first (Matthew 28:5–6), and Manoah pleaded with the Lord that He would send the angel again and teach Manoah and his wife what they should do unto the child that would be born unto them. (See Judges 13:8.) There are many other scriptures that support this ability of angels. (See 2 Kings 1:15, 2 Kings 1:3–5, Daniel 7:15–16; 8:15–16; 9:21–23; 11:2–12:13.)

In Galatians 1:8, Paul warns that if an angel from heaven preaches any other gospel that the apostles had not preached let him be accursed. Paul, understanding the reality of angels' teaching, warns that the saints must not heed to an angel preaching any other gospel contrary to the gospel preached by the apostles. The Greek verb εὐαγγελίζω (ĕvängĕlēzō) means to proclaim the Word of God through preaching or teaching. According to this Greek verb the view of Paul is that angels have the very ability to proclaim the gospel through preaching or teaching. It was this reason that Paul warned of deceptions that would occur. Paul recognized that fallen angels can come and proclaim the gospel too. He was warning that all angels who come to a person may not be good angels. Some may be fallen angels coming to deceive people with false doctrine.

Paul gave the Galatians a manner to distinguish a good angel from an evil angel in Galatians 1:8. Evil angels will pervert the gospel. They will proclaim a gospel that the apostles did not preach or teach. On the other hand, the angels of God will never speak anything contrary to the Word of God. (See Galatians 1:8.) For this reason, if an angel comes and speaks things contrary to the Word of God, a person must not obey him, but let him—the angel—be accursed. The angel is not of God, but of Satan.

Exodus 23:20–23, Luke 1:11–20, and Genesis 19:1–26 reveal that an angel of God must be obeyed by a person lest that person be punished for not obeying. Nevertheless, this is true as long as an angel follows the will of God and does not do things that are contrary to the Word of God. Only a godly angel must be obeyed. A fallen angel must be rejected and not heeded.

In 1 John 4:1–3, John warns the saints not to believe every spirit, but to test the spirits. The test given by John centers around whether or not Christ came in the flesh. What does this mean? A person will not be of God if he denies the incarnation, the passion, the bodily resurrection of Christ, the ascension of Christ, or the fact that Christ still remains in the flesh. If an angel confesses that Christ came in the flesh, he is of God; but if an angel confesses that Christ did not come in the flesh, he is of Satan.

Angels Can Bury a Dead Body

According to Jude 9, when the chief angel Michael fought over the body of Moses, he did not bring forth a blasphemous condemnation against Satan but simply said, "The Lord rebuke you." In studying Jude 9, many connect it to the resurrection of Moses from the dead. But this is not what is meant at all. It is universally agreed that what Jude mentions here is drawn from an incident mentioned in the book entitled *The Assumption of Moses*. In other words, Jude draws as his source about this situation that truly occurred between Michael and Satan, from a book called *The Assumption of Moses*.

The reason Jude used this information was because it possessed a correct view of this history. In *The Assumption of Moses* the series of events that occurred after the death of Moses are as follows:

- God ordered Michael to bury the dead body of Moses so that no man could know where it was buried.

- Satan opposed this simply because he had power over death. For this reason, the dead body of Moses is rightly his property.

- Satan also opposed this because Moses was a murderer having killed an Egyptian.

- Michael charged Satan with having instigated the serpent to tempt Eve.

- Satan ceased his opposition over Michael burying the dead body of Moses.

- The soul of Moses was carried into paradise beneath the surface of the earth.

- The dead body of Moses was buried in the recesses of the mountains.

From this, Moses was still dead and had not been resurrected. Jude is only referring to the truth that Moses' dead body was buried. Accordingly, the incident brought up in Jude 9 took place after the death of Moses. Satan claimed the dead body of Moses. However, God, through Michael, intervened and buried it in the land of Moab to keep it from the Jewish people. (See Deuteronomy 34:5–6.) If the dead body of Moses were resurrected it had to be resurrected in the permanent resurrection since his body went through corruption. And this was impossible. Why? Christ is the firstfruit of the permanent resurrection (John 20:17–20; 1

Corinthians 15:20–23; Hebrews 2:14–15) and Moses could not then be the first of this type of resurrection. (See John 20:17–20; 1 Corinthians 15:20–23; Hebrews 2:14–15.) Moses was not resurrected before Christ in this permanent resurrection.

Studying Jude 9 carefully, it must be understood that the word *body* comes from the Greek noun σῶμα (sōmä). This Greek noun has reference here to a dead body, not a living body. It is also used to denote a dead body in other references. (See Matthew 14:12; 27:52, 58–59; Hebrews 13:11.) There are several reasons God buried the dead body of Moses through the means of Michael instead of allowing the Jews to bury it:

- If the Jews had buried the dead body of Moses, then at a time of sin they would have dug it up and would have worshiped it.

- The Jews may have also worshiped the gravesite and designated it as a shrine directing their prayers to Moses rather than to God.

- The Gentiles may have chosen it as a site for idol worship.

- If the Jews had known the burial site, they may have been persuaded at times of persecution to pray to Moses so that he would intervene on their behalf to God.

- The gravesite radiates a holiness that is too great for any mortal to experience and live.

- This was part of the punishment that God declared unto Moses in not reacting as fast as he should have done in the sin of Baal-Peor. (See Numbers 25:1–18; 31:16.)

Deuteronomy 34:5–7 and Joshua 1:1–2 prove that Moses did die. Deuteronomy 34:5–7 bears witness to the fact that the dead body of Moses was buried. But by whom? The Masoretic Hebrew text says that "He" buried the dead body of Moses while the Greek Septuagint says "They" buried the dead body of Moses.

In the Masoretic Hebrew text the focus is on the fact that God ordered the burial of Moses' body. It was His order alone. In the Greek Septuagint, the focus is on God and Michael. God is the one who ordered the burial of Moses' body while Michael was the one that carried it out. Two parts of one whole truth.

On that account, both the Lord and Michael had a part in the burial of Moses. So, Jude is confirmed to be accurate by the Greek Septugaint and *The Assumption of Moses.*

According to the Palestinian Targum, Michael was involved in the burial of the body of Moses through the order of the Lord God. (See Deuteronomy 34:6.)

CHAPTER 9

Other Angelic Facts Commonly Known

Angels Exist

THE SCRIPTURES NEVER deny the existence of angels but always attest their existence. (See Genesis 17:7–12; Judges 13:1–21; Matthew 28:2–4; Jude 6; Daniel 7:10; 10:1–21; Luke 20:35; Genesis 18–19.) From the scriptures, there are frequently seen beings that are beyond human limitations, have a spiritual nature, do many works for God, and are sent by God as His messengers, allies, teachers, and agents to fulfill His will. The constant appearance of angels performing acts and deeds that go beyond human capacity would be without force or meaning if the angels did not exist. If the angels can be doubted as existing and doing such acts and deeds, the men who existed and performed acts as recorded in Scripture must as well be doubted. Most who deny the existence of angels accept without any question the reality of the men spoken of in Scripture. So when there is interaction between angels and men, the reality of one cannot be accepted without accepting the reality of the other. If a person rejects the reality of one, he must reject the reality of the other. Therefore, by rejecting the existence of angels, a long and evil course of trying to dismantle all of Scripture and everything written therein will begin.

Does anyone reject the testimony of Moses about the existence of angels? What about the many testimonies mentioned in Scripture that proclaim the existence of angels? Does anyone reject all these when these testimonies are more valuable than any other critic today? Throughout the Scriptures great testimonies are given on the existence of angels. Many of these testimonies come from the wicked. These witnesses on the existence of angels are more reliable than any modern critic. Why? These persons had not a hidden agenda behind what they declared, but only spoke the truth. From all the witnesses to the existence of angels, no greater witness can be given about the reality of God's angels than Christ. While upon the earth Christ taught about the existence of God's angels. Christ being God speaks with undeniable authority that what He spoke was the truth. Christ spoke about the existence of angels in many places. (See Luke 22:1, 18, 30; Matthew 18:10–11; 22:29–30; 24:31; 25:31–32; 25:41; 26:53; Luke 15:7–10; 20:35–36; 22:43; and Mark 12:25.)

The angels of God were involved in the Old Testament and its covenants, and in the New Testament and its covenant. The Old Testament and New Testament represent God's angels as spiritual beings who are as real as human beings and as real as God Himself. They show, in as much detail as God allows, their nature, works, and other important facts. Most doctrines gradually progress in their development in Scripture, but the doctrine of angels is found at almost the beginning of Scripture, at the end, and almost everywhere else between.

From the very conception of Christianity, the belief in angels was present so much so that to dismantle it from Christianity would cause untold damage. So much about the doctrine of angels is connected to Christianity that no one can well take it away without unraveling Christianity from its connection to the supernatural.

The early leaders of the church usually recognized the value in believing that angels do exist. The following points uncover the value in believing in the existence of angels:

- It makes common sense to accept the existence of angels since God says that they do exist.

- Accepting the existence of angels keeps Christianity in uniformity.

- The belief in angels becomes a safeguard against having a narrow thought regarding Creation.

- The belief in angels helps us have a correct conception of Christ since Christ is superior to all angels.

- The belief in angels gives us a glimpse into the supernatural realm.

- The belief in angels gives us a greater view of God's mercies.

- The belief in angels gives us insight into the state that the saints will obtain.

- The belief in angels and their power humbles us. Why? God's angels have never sinned and have never been in a state of sin while the saints are only saved sinners.

Angels Stand Before the Lord

On occasion, God's angels stand before the Lord God. Since the occasions change, the times that God's angels stand before the Lord also change. Not all angels stand before the Lord God at once, but angels stand before God consecutively whether individually or in groups.

First Kings 22:19 concerns Micaiah—a prophet of the Most High God—where he beheld a great phenomenon that was bewildering to the sight. The prophet saw the Lord sitting on His throne and the host of heaven standing before Him on the right and left sides. The term *host of heaven* is an expression that often has reference to the planets, stars, galaxies, solar systems, and whatever else remains in the heavenlies. (See Jeremiah 8:2; Isaiah 34:4; Acts 7:42.) Yet, it is also an expression that concerns angels, fallen angels, and demons. What does this event that Micaiah saw mean? It reveals that God on occasion, with His heavenly hosts, holds conferences concerning the affairs of humanity. On these occasions and others God's angels stand before Him.

Another record of a heavenly conference was when the hosts appeared before the Lord God. (See Job 1:6 and 2:1.) In this instance, Satan was present and sought to prove that Job only served God because of what God had given him in blessings. This great conference was only held because of one man. The same thing is also seen in 1 Kings 22:19 where a heavenly conference was held to deliberate on Ahab.

In Matthew 18:10, the doctrine that each person has at least one angel assigned to him is well proven. In this passage, chief angels as guardians over individual lives periodically stand before God and plead the case of these individuals before Him.

What is the purpose of the angels standing before God? They worship, praise, and exalt the Lord God. They receive answers to the prayers of the saints, and they receive instructions from God on what to do and how to do it. They ask the Lord God for help in certain situations in which they find themselves, and they ask the Lord God for assistance in certain parts of creation. They beseech the Lord God for assistance in the lives of individuals and inform the Lord God about the affairs of humanity, the earth, and all creation. They refute the accusations of Satan and his forces against the saints.

Angels Are Subject to Christ

The Book of 1 Peter 3:22 relates to the resurrection, exaltation, and glorification of Christ as man. Therefore, 1 Peter 3:22 shows that before Christ's incarnation, all angels, whether unfallen or fallen, and demons were subject to Christ. However, when His voluntary subordinate state commenced upon the earth, this subjection ended. Why? Christ as God gave up the free use of certain divine attributes, though retaining them, so that He could be a perfect example to all mankind. (See Philippians 2:5–7.) This subjection was again renewed at the exaltation and glorification of Christ as man still being in the incarnated state after His resurrection.

Paul in Hebrews gives several reasons why Christ, even in His incarnated state, is higher than the angels:

- Christ's inheritance (Hebrews 1:4)

- Christ obtained a more excellent name (Hebrews 1:4)

- He is the Son of God (Hebrews 1:5)

- Angels worship Christ (Hebrews 1:6)

- Christ is the Creator of the angels (Hebrews 1:7–8; Colossians 1:16)

- Christ is one member of the Godhead (Hebrews 1:8)

- Christ as God is eternal, not created (Hebrews 1:8)

- Christ is an eternal King (Hebrews 1:8)

- Christ is God the Father's only anointed One—Messiah (Hebrews 1:9)

- Christ is the Creator of the universe (Hebrews 1:10)

- Christ's divine nature (Hebrews 1:8–12)

- Christ is the Renewer of creation (Hebrews 1:10–11)

- His creative power and eternity (Hebrews 1:8–12)

- Christ is the exalted One (Hebrews1:13)

- Christ is the Director of the angels (Hebrews 1:14)

- Rejecting Christ's word brings greater punishment than rejecting the words of angels (Hebrews 2:1–3)

- Christ has a greater confirmation of word (Hebrews 2:3–4)

- A better covenant (Hebrews 2:1–4)

- Christ is a greater conqueror than the angels (Hebrews 2:5, 8)

- Christ has greater power than the angels (Hebrews 2:6–7)

- War against all rebels and their final conquest (Hebrews 2:5–8)

- Christ is greater in humility than the angels (Hebrews 2:9)

- Christ is greater in glory and honor than the angels (Hebrews 2:9)

- He created all created things (Hebrews 2:10)

- Christ is the Redeemer of man (Hebrews 2:10)

- Christ was perfect through sufferings (Hebrews 2:10)

- Christ is the Sanctifier of men (Hebrews 2:11)

- Christ became a Brother to men (Hebrews 2:11–13)

- Christ became the Preacher of God's name to men (Hebrews 2:12)

- Christ became the Singer in the midst of the church (Hebrews 2:12)

- Christ became perfect trust in God (Hebrews 2:13)

- Christ adopts children to God the Father (Hebrews 2:13)

- Christ partook of the human nature (Hebrews 2:14)

- His conquest of Sheol-Hades and death (Hebrews 2:14–15)

- Christ died to destroy death (Hebrews 2:14)

- Christ's exaltation (Hebrews 1:13–14)

- Christ conquered Satan (Hebrews 2:14)

- Christ delivered the righteous souls from paradise (Hebrews 2:15)

- Christ was like men, except by sin (Hebrews 2:16–17)

- Christ suffered temptation and won, so He could help those who are tempted (Hebrews 2:18)

The Angels' Home Is Heaven

The home of God's angels is not the first heaven, the earth, or the second heaven, but the third heaven. (See 2 Corinthians 12:1–4.) Most angels do not permanently reside there. They are doing the will of God throughout the universe. Many angels are often seen in the second heaven, first heaven, and the earth. These, though occasionally, do return to their home for a time and afterward return to their missions in other parts of God's kingdom.

From Scripture, other certain facts about heaven are seen:

- ◆ Its location. According to Isaiah 14:12–15, heaven is in the northern part of the universe. A telescopic camera used to view this area reveals an empty space where no stars, planets, solar systems, or galaxies are found. It is this place where heaven is found.

- ◆ Its shape. According to Job 22:14, Psalm 19:6, Isaiah 40:22 and Ecclesiastes 11:6, heaven is circular in shape.

- ◆ Its nature. Heaven is spiritual.

- ◆ Since its shape is that of a circle, some have thought that it may be seen to be like a planet, but spiritually rather than physically. (See Nehemiah 9:6; Genesis 1:1; 2:1.)

- ◆ It is called a better country. (See Hebrews 11:10–16.)

- ◆ It has real cities, palaces, a paradise, foundations, tabernacle, and whatever else God needs or desires. (See Romans 1:20; Hebrews 11:10–15; John 14:1–3; Revelation 2:7; 16:1; 21:2–3; 22:2, 14; Job 38:4–7.)

According to Revelation 12:7–9, Satan and his angels reside in the second heaven. According to Isaiah 14:12–15, Satan and all his angels were thrown out of the third heaven as their home due to their attack upon it. Yet on occasions fallen angels can enter the first heaven or come on the earth when they are specifically needed. They can even come into God's heaven. (See Job 1:6; 2:1; Revelation 12:10–12.)

The main abode of Satan and his angels is the second heaven while the main abode of demons is the first heaven and the earth. (See 1 Kings 22:19–23.) Demons are the ones who almost exclusively infest the first heaven and the earth. Demons on occasion can enter the second heaven and even the third heaven, but this is rarely done. (See 1 Kings 22:22–23.) Why? Their place is in the first heaven and the earth.

Angels Make Oaths

In Daniel 12:5–7, the man clothed in fine linen, who is Gabriel, swears by Him who lives forever that the fulfillment of God's mystery will continue during the last half of the Tribulation and beyond. The very fact that this person swears not by himself proves that this person cannot be God.

God, when making an oath, swears by no one but Himself. (See Hebrews 6:13; Isaiah 62:8; Jeremiah 22:5; 49:13; 51:14; Amos 6:8.) Consequently, by this person swearing by the Lord, it shows that it is not the Lord who appeared to Daniel, but an angel, Gabriel. Swearing by the name of the deity or by God has always been considered the most sacred and solemn affirmation of a statement. It is simply calling God to witness that which has been said is the sacred truth. Gabriel appears in Revelation 10:6 to make a similar oath having reference to the same thing.

Angels Appear Unaware

In Hebrews 12:2, Paul warns that some who have been hospitable to strangers have in essence entertained angels and not realized it. Paul means that angels can appear in absolute flesh before humans, with the humans being unaware of their identity. Paul could not help but draw proof of his argument from the Old Testament. In the Old Testament, angels appeared in absolute flesh before unsuspecting persons who consciously did not know that the angels were present. There are several passages that Paul must have had in mind. (See Genesis 19:1–26; Judges 6:11–22; 13:6–23.) These passages were used to prove that saints must be compassionate to strangers since those strangers may truly be angels in disguise. Genesis 18:2–33 cannot be placed in these passages since Abraham consciously knew that he was entertaining the Lord God and two angels.

God's Enemies Tormented Before Angels

According to Revelation 14:9–10, all persons who worship the Antichrist will be cast into the Lake of Fire and forever be tormented before the angels. Those creatures found in the Lake of Fire will be able to be seen by God the Father, God the Son known as the Lamb, God the Holy Spirit, the angels of God, the saints of God, and the natural inhabitants of the earth. The angels, the saints, and the natural inhabitants will all be able to behold sinners tormented in the Lake of Fire. This will be an everlasting monument of God vindicating His holiness against sin. (See Isaiah 66:22–24.) Since the Lake of Fire is not physical and belongs to the spiritual realm, then the means by which the natural inhabitants can see the Lake of Fire is through spiritual means.

While many will have incorruptible and immortal bodies due to the second resurrection (Daniel 12:3; John 5:28–29; Revelation 20:4–6), in the Lake of Fire they will never be allowed the privilege to materialize them into the physical realm. Why? The fire in the Lake of Fire is spiritual fire and cannot hurt or torment physical bodies but only spiritual bodies or those bodies present in the spiritual realm through transformation.

Resurrected bodies are physical bodies that become similar to spiritual bodies. Since these bodies become like spiritual bodies, they can materialize in the spiritual realm and the physical realm. However, this ability will be taken away from the bodies in the Lake of Fire. Therefore, these bodies will forever remain a part of the spiritual realm and will never materialize into the physical realm. This is also true of the spiritual bodies of fallen angels.

Revelation 14:9–10 is just one passage that proves the eternal torment of the wicked. (See Isaiah 66:22–24; Daniel 12:2; Jude 6–7; Revelation 20:10–15; 21:8; 22:15.)

Angels Recognize the Importance of the Blood

In Exodus 12:7–12, an angel of God recognizes this very fact by only killing the firstborn of those not having their posts covered with the blood of the sacrifice. To the angel of God, the blood represented God's atonement and the canceling of God's wrath upon those inhabitants who had the posts of their houses covered. In other words, the shedding of blood prohibited the angel from carrying out God's wrath to all inhabitants of Egypt. Why? Where the shedding of blood occurred there appeared God's atonement. The blood cancelled God's wrath and judgment upon the occupants of those houses due only to God's acceptance of the blood. (See Ephesians 4:10; Hebrews 10:10–12; Exodus 30:12.) The blood of the lamb divided those who were of God and those who were not. So, it was a dividing line that separated the godly from the ungodly.

The reason the destroying angel understood that the blood represented the atonement was because "without blood there was no remission of sin." (See Hebrews 9:22.) However, the destroying angel also recognized that the blood represented God's ownership, God's protecting power, God's purifying power, God's saving power, and God's cleansing power as well. (See 1 Peter 1:2; Hebrews 11:28; 12:24; Romans 6:15–23.)

Angels Can Measure Things

In Revelation 21:17, an angel measures the length of New Jerusalem. Further, in Ezekiel 40:1–46:24 Ezekiel is shown the Millennial Temple and what pertained to it. He is shown also that it will be built near the earthly Jerusalem in what will be called the "Holy Oblation." (See Isaiah 2:2–4; 35:8; Ezekiel 37:26; 45:1–5; 48:10, 20–21.) In Ezekiel 40:1–42:20, an angel measures certain parts of the Millennial Temple several times. The reason the angel shows Ezekiel the Millennial Temple in precise terms is because God wants the Jewish people to never forget that there will be a temple built near earthly Jerusalem by God Himself. (See Zechariah 6:12–13.) God also does not want them to forget that their God will reside there on His earthly throne forever. (See Ezekiel 43:7.)

Daniel 9:24 reads from the Greek Septuagint, "The Holy of Holies will forever be appreciated by your people." The idea expressed by Gabriel in this part of Daniel 9:24 is that the Jewish people do not appreciate the Holy of Holies. Why? Their rebellious nature and desire to rebel against God. The Holy of Holies may be reckoned as a banner, waving back and forth before the Jewish people telling them not to sin. The Holy of Holies was an open and visible deterrent against evil and sin. The Holy of Holies is forever a symbol of holiness in its purest form.

It will only be when the rebellion of the Jewish people ceases that they will rejoice in the Holy of Holies and appreciate it. The end of their rebellion will occur after the Second Coming when they are judged again. (See Zephaniah 3:11; Isaiah 1:28–31; 8:20–22; 27:9; 59:20; 65:11–15; Zechariah 12:10–14.)

The word *forever* settles the question whether there will be a temple forever on the earth. There will be. This falls in line with Ezekiel 43:7, concerning the Millennial Temple. Ezekiel 43:7 establishes the fact that the Millennial Temple, and the Holy of Holies as part of it, will forever exist. It will be the place of Christ's earthly throne forever. God the Father will have His throne in two places as will Christ: one in the Millennial Temple, and one in New Jerusalem. (See Revelation 22:1–5; Ezekiel 43:7.) The thrones for God the Father and Christ found in the New Jerusalem were never situated in the temple of New Jerusalem. Psalm 11:4 shows that the temple and the thrones are different things, neither being in one nor the other.

Apparently, the reason John saw no temple in New Jerusalem after the restoration of the earth and the heavens is because:

- God the Father and the Lamb will at that point be the temple of New Jerusalem. This means that they will be the center of interest or attention.

- The Millennial Temple will forever be the earthly temple and will forever be sufficient for temple matters.

- New Jerusalem's temple will become combined with the Millennial Temple. It will be taken out of New Jerusalem and will forever exist as part of the Millennial Temple. (See Psalm 11:4; Revelation 3:12; 4–5; 11:19; 14:17; 16:17; 21:2; 21:10; John 14:1–3; Hebrews 9:11; 11:10–16; 12:22.)

- The temple in New Jerusalem must be taken out of New Jerusalem and become a very important part of the Millennial Temple. This is based upon Greek grammar in Revelation 21:22.

It is the Millennial Temple in which the overcomer will be made a pillar. Earthly Jerusalem will continue to exist. The name of God will forever be upon earthly Jerusalem. Earthly Jerusalem will forever be the seat of earthly government, the world's capital, and center of worship since the Millennial Temple will forever be by it. (See 2 Chronicles 33:4–7; 1 Chronicles 23:25; 2 Kings 21:7; Ezekiel 34:1–35; 40:1–46:24; 48; 43:7; Isaiah 2:2–4; 11:11–12:6; 33:10; 65:18; Joel 3:17–20; Micah 4:7; Zechariah 8:3–23; 14:1–21; 15:1–18.)

CHAPTER 10

Other Angelic Facts Less Known

Christ Will Confess the Overcomers to the Angels

IN REVELATION 3:5, a great promise is given to the saints. The promise is that the one who overcomes will be clothed in white, will not have his name blotted out of the Book of Life, and will have his name confessed before God the Father and before the holy angels.

In Revelation 2:17, the Greek verb νικάω (nēkäō) is used to express the inheritance of the saints, their obtaining it, and their overcoming all the things in the world that tried to destroy their state of holiness and grace and keep them from finishing the race of faith to obtain unconditional eternal life. (See 1 Corinthians 9:24–27; Hebrews 12:1–3; 1 Timothy 6:2; 2 Timothy 4:7; Galatians 2:2; 5:7; Revelation 2:26, 3:5, 3:12, 3:21, and 21:7.) Therefore, the overcomer is one who has finished the race of his faith, has obtained unconditional eternal life, been exalted, been glorified, been resurrected, and has received his inheritance. This will begin at the Rapture.

The promise brought up about the overcomers and God's angels is that Christ will confess them before the angels. Why? The overcomers kept their salvation, kept their course, finished their race, and never gave up or gave in to the state of sin.

The Church Can Teach the Angels Wisdom

The ignorance of the angels about the plan of salvation is well attested. Even the chief-adversary of God was ignorant of the plan of salvation. So ignorant was Satan and all his forces about the plan of salvation that the ancient fathers of the church could not help but write about this very important fact. For example, Ignatius writes about this fact:

> Now the virginity of Mary was hidden from the prince of this world, as was also her offspring, and the death of the Lord; three mysteries of renown, which were wrought in silence, but have been revealed to us.[1]

Again, Ignatius discusses this subject, and writes about Satan and his ignorance:

> For many things are unknown to thee [Satan]: [such as the following]: the virginity of Mary; the wonderful birth; Who it was that became incarnate; the star which guided those who were in the east; the Magi who presented gifts; the salutation of the archangel to the Virgin; the marvelous conception of her that was betrothed; the announcement of the boy-forerunner respecting the son of the Virgin, and his leaping in the womb on account of what was foreseen; the songs of the angels over him that was born; the glad tidings announced to the shepherds; the fear of Herod lest his kingdom should be taken from him; the command to slay the infants; the removal into Egypt, and the return from that country to the same region; the infant swaddling-bands; the human registration; the nourishing by means of milk; the name of father given to him who did not beget; the manger because there was not room [elsewhere]; no human preparation [for the child]; the gradual growth, human speech, hunger, thirst, journeying, weariness; the offering of sacrifices, and then also circumcision, baptism; the voice of God over him that was baptized, as to who He was and whence [He had come]; the testimony of the Spirit and the Father from above; the voice of John the prophet when it signified the passion by the appellation of the "Lamb"; the performance of divers miracles, manifold healings; the rebuke of the Lord ruling both the sea and the winds; the evil spirits expelled; thou thyself subjected to torture, and when afflicted by the power of him who had been

manifested, not having it in thy power to do anything. Seeing these things, thou wast in utter perplexity.[2]

Such was the ignorance of Satan and all his evil forces about Christ that they willingly moved toward the undoing of themselves. Their defeat occurred by them wanting Christ's death on the Cross. If they had only known that the death of Christ would have been their undoing, they would have never wanted and pushed for His death. In fact, they would have tried everything possible to keep Him alive. Undeniably, Ignatius concluded that Satan, recognizing that through the Cross his destruction would be gained, attempted to put a stop to its erection, but he failed.[3]

With Satan and all his evil forces being ignorant about the plan of salvation, the angels of God also, up to a point, were kept in the dark. Generally, the angels of God know about the plan of salvation. However, in a strict sense, God put them in the dark as it related to the plan of salvation. Every detail that was and is part of the plan of salvation was only known in the counsels and designs of the Godhead. This caused the plan of salvation to be a mystery. (See Romans 1:1–5; 16:25; 1 Corinthians 2:9–16; Ephesians 3:1–8; Hebrews 8:6.) Therefore, the angels of God only know about the plan of salvation in a summarized version. They have never fully comprehended what it was and what it is. They can only understand certain parts of this plan. Above all, the fact that the angels of God are ignorant of every detail about the plan of salvation is well confirmed by them wanting to look into the plan of salvation. If they understood it in a very strict sense, they would not desire to understand it.

Further, the fact that the church teaches angels wisdom also shows that God's angels are still ignorant up to a point about the plan of salvation. The angels of God still cannot fully comprehend the reason Christ went through all of His sufferings for humanity. They earnestly want to understand this by studying the church and what benefits and consequences are caused in the lives of the saints by this great work of God. It is this reason the saints are seen as a spectacle before the spiritual realm. (See 1 Corinthians 4:9.)

The wisdom that the angels seek and the church teaches is all things about the plan of salvation. Nevertheless, Ephesians 3:10 cannot be limited to the angels of God. Why? The church is also teaching Satan and all the evil forces about the mystery of redemption.

Angels are Countless in Number

In Hebrews 12:22, Paul sees the number of the angels as numberless, while in Revelation 5:11 John saw 10,000 times 10,000 and thousands and thousands of angels. If we calculate this, after the rebellion of Satan, the angels of God number 100 trillion in number (10,000 x 10,000 = 100,000,000 x 1,000 = 100,000,000,000 x 1,000 = 100,000,000,000,000). Before the rebellion of Satan, the angels of God numbered more than 150 trillion. This is seen from the fact that one third of God's angels who rebelled are still loose. Some of those who rebelled have been confined in Tartarus due to the diabolical acts that they did. (See Revelation 12:7–9; 2 Peter 2:4; Jude 6–8; Genesis 6:1–4.) So, more than one third of God's angels rebelled against Him, and at least one hundred trillion remained true and obedient.

Only John was given the number of angels, not Paul or any other writer of Scripture. Yet, this number is so enormous that no man can count it. So, the angels are still countless in number. Men are unable to number them. The only One who can calculate their number is the One who created them, and that One is God. John did not have this ability.

Angels Carry Weapons and Are in Armies

In 1 Chronicles 21:16 and 21:27–28, David beheld in a vision an angel of the Lord having a sword first drawn and then later put back into its sheath. Again, an angel is seen with a sword in Numbers 22:22–35.

Angels carrying weapons did not surprise the ancients at all. The angels carry these weapons in the judgments of God and in conflicts. The ancients saw spiritual beings whom God equipped in their creation so they could use weapons in many respects like the human race.

Often, humans underestimate the capacity of God's angels. The notion that they are unable to carry weapons is one of these instances.

What kind of weapons do God's angels use? The weapons employed by God's angels for use in carrying out God's will and mission are ancient oriented. (See 1 Chronicles 21:16, 27–30; Numbers 22:22–35.) All the evidence proves that weapons used by God's angels are those that are similar to those used by the ancients. The very notion that presents itself here is that before humanity invented the sword, the angels of God and fallen angels were already using them. The same logic follows with all other ancient weapons.

The weapons used by spiritual beings are similar in appearance to those weapons used by the ancients. However, these weapons are supernatural in nature with ability that is beyond human comprehension. Remember that an angel smote and killed 185,000 Assyrians in a single night. (See 2 Chronicles 32:21; 2 Kings 19:35.) The thought expressed here in Scripture is that the angel used a supernatural sword to commit these slayings, and he killed them all with one single strike. There were not 185,000 strikes of the sword by the angel, but only one. This proves the supernatural nature of the sword used by the angel.

Demons, being disembodied spirits, cannot carry weapons. However, by their supernatural power, they can move these weapons at will without having to hold them.

The Scriptures prove beyond a doubt that the angels of God are organized into angelic armies. (See Revelation 12:7–9; 19; Zechariah 14:13; Daniel 7:7–14; Joshua 5:13–15.) What tactical system are the angelic armies using? The angels of God, fallen angels, and even demons use in their armies the tactical system known as Legion. (See Matthew 26:53; Mark 5:9; 5:15; Luke 8:30.) The opposing forces in gigantic battles and wars employ this to gain victory and areas of control. These gigantic conflicts are fought throughout the second heaven, first heaven, and even on the earth. From what is known about the Legion used by the Romans and the evidence found from the Scriptures, the overwhelming notion is that before the Romans used this tactical system, angels, fallen angels, and demons had been using it since the rebellion of Satan. The form of the legion used by the Romans was and is the same form used by angels and demons to fight gigantic conflicts. Further, there are spiritual armies in conflict throughout the second heaven, first heaven, and on the earth. There are gigantic battles and wars arranged as legions. From the information uncovered, the gigantic conflicts are carried out like those the Romans fought. However, usually the opponents of the Romans did not use the Legion tactical system but another kind. The opposing sides in the spiritual realm both employ the legion tactical system.

It must be said that the conflicts fought in the spiritual realm by just a few opponents are not gigantic, but individual. This distinction is noteworthy. With individual conflicts, the legion tactical system is not employed, but with gigantic conflicts, it is.

Angels Are Not to Be Worshiped

Cults place more emphasis on angels or demons than on Christ. During the life of Paul, angelic cults were prominent. This prompted Paul to declare often that Christ was greater than the angels. This was done to signify that Christ is not an angel, but God. Because of the prevalence of angelic cults, Paul warns against worshiping angels. It is pure idolatry since only God must be worshiped. (See Colossians 2:18; Matthew 4:10; Exodus 34:14; Psalm 81:9; Revelation 19:10; 22:8–9.) Also, John, by his example, declares the worship of angels is forbidden. (See Revelation 22:8–9.) Why? They are servants of the Lord God.

Although angels are forbidden to be worshiped, they can be thanked for being sent by God to help us. This is shown to be true from Daniel 4:37, according to the Greek Septuagint. With the fact that angels are forbidden to be worshiped comes two other truths. The first truth is that angels must not be prayed to. Christ does not pray to the angels, but to God. (See Matthew 6:9–13; 26:53; 1 Timothy 2:5; 2 Samuel 7:27; 1 Kings 8:28; 2 Kings 19:4; 20:5.) The second truth is that the images of angels are forbidden to be made. (See Exodus 20:4–5.) Why? Idolatry would be practiced through these images. Further, a curse is placed upon anyone who makes an image like this.

Angels Were Tested in Their Own Dispensation

Humanity is in the Dispensation of Grace now. (See Ephesians 3:2.) This began at the end of John the Baptist's ministry and the beginning of Christ's ministry and will continue until Christ's Second Coming with other signs beforehand. (See Mark 1:1–14; Matthew 11:11–13; John 1:16–17.) Before that dispensation and others, there was a Dispensation of Angels. The Dispensation of Angels was a time when angels were given rulership over all creation under God to administer His will and desire. (See Genesis 1:1–2; Job 4:18; 15:15; Isaiah 14:12–15; Ezekiel 28:12–19; Matthew 25:41; 1 Peter 3:22.)

A dispensation is a probationary period that God employs to test free moral agents in respect to a specific manner that has been or could have been used to see if they will remain true and obedient to Him.

The length of this time was from the creation of time to the rebellion of Satan and his failed invasion of God's heaven. This brought forth the utter ruin of God's creation, to a certain extent, because of God's judgment falling upon all creation. (See Genesis 1:1–2; Job 4:18; 15:15; Isaiah 14:12–15; Ezekiel 28:12–19; Matthew 25:41; 1 Peter 3:22.)

From what has already been learned, some very interesting facts are uncovered:

- The angels were given rulership over all of God's creation to administer His will and desire. As such, the angels ruled over God's creation under God's constitution and manifesto, which means that they could only rule by the precepts that God had given them.

- Satan rebelled because he wanted all of God's creation as his own.

- Angels lost their rulership over all creation due to the fall of Satan and his angels. Why? No angel had a tempter. It was this fact that separated the fall of the angels from the fall of humanity. It is this reason God gave humanity another chance through accepting Christ as their Savior to be destined to regain their rulership over God's creation while not giving the angels another chance.

- The main purpose of Satan in tempting humanity to sin was to gain, for his own sake, rulership over all of God's creation.

- Satan's plan worked and he received rulership over all of God's creation.

- Satan was a usurper of what God had for humanity since the angels, having no tempter, lost their rulership over all creation.

- The elect angels suffered much by humanity's fall.

- When Christ came on the scene He, by His redemptive work, took back from Satan the rulership of all created things.

Though it had a favorable beginning, the Dispensation of Angels ended in utter failure. God created Satan, all creatures, and all things perfect and without sin. (See Ecclesiastes 3:11; Ezekiel 28:12–19.) So, evil came into being by sinless, free-will creatures rebelling against God.

In this dispensation, the purpose of God was to test angels to see if they would rebel against Him or continue to be obedient to Him. It is for this reason that God tests humanity. His purpose is the same for testing any free moral agent. (See John 8:44; Ephesians 3:9–10; 1 Timothy 5:21; 1 John 5:18–19; Jude 6–7.) The test was simple: to be subject to God and obey Him in all that He commanded. Satan and his forces did not achieve, but failed miserably because of their own ambitions, will, and pride.

In this dispensation, provision was made for those angels who remained true and obedient to God and fought in the gigantic war caused by Satan's rebellion. What was the provision? These angels who remained steadfast in piety and obedience to their Lord obtained a sure and certain knowledge of their eternal safety and freedom from the possibility of ever falling from grace. God confirmed His angels as holy, righteous, still in the state of grace, and free from the very possibility of ever falling. It is this reason that Paul, in 1 Timothy 5:21, called God's angels "elect angels." *Elect* denotes that after the rebellion of Satan those who did not rebel were confirmed by God as still being His holy angels.

St. Augustine writes:

> Whilst some of the angels, then, in their pride and impiety rebelled against God, and were cast down from their heavenly abode into the lowest darkness, the remaining number dwelt with God in eternal and unchanging purity and happiness. For all were not sprung from one angel who had fallen and been condemned, so that they were not all, like men, involved by one original sin in the bonds of an inherited guilt, and so made subject to the penalty which one had incurred; but when he, who afterwards became the devil, was with his associates in crime exalted in pride, and by that very exaltation was with them cast down, the rest remained steadfast in piety and obedience to their Lord, and obtained, what they had not enjoyed, a sure and certain knowledge of their eternal safety, and freedom from the possibility of falling.[4]

Therefore, God doubtless confirms the angels who stood with Him as holy, righteous, still in the state of grace, and free from the very possibility of ever falling.

How are they confirmed? The sight of the terrible defeat and destruction of Satan's attempt to overthrow God and the consequences brought upon Satan and all his followers confirm them. The main consequence was and is that those who rebelled are destined for eternal punishment in the Lake of Fire. Also, through finding, experiencing, and uncovering their position and state compared with the position and state of those who rebelled, they are again confirmed. Further, the work of redemption and Christ's ascension confirms them. (See Ephesians 3:10; 1 Timothy 3:16; 1 Peter 1:12.)

Since the rebellion of Satan and his followers, the elect angels are completely dependent on Christ for unconditional eternal life. (See Revelation 2:7; Psalm 103:20; 104:4; Hebrews 1:13–14.) Why? For the following reasons:

- Christ was and is the Savior of the elect angels by His grace. Though Christ did not save them as He does men, Christ did save the elect angels from the eternal punishment that they were in great danger of and otherwise would have fallen into with the other angels. (See Matthew 25:41; 2 Peter 2:4; Jude 6–7; Revelation 20:11–15; Isaiah 14:12–15; 66:22–24.) The point here is that all angels were in great danger of reaping eternal punishment in the Lake of Fire if the grace of Christ had not intervened for the obedient angels.

- The elect angels were and are dependent on the sovereign grace of Christ to sustain them in their state of grace and keep them from falling like Satan and his angels.

- Christ is their judge (John 5:22).

- The elect angels receive as their reward unconditional eternal life by means of Christ.

- The elect angels have their happiness in Christ due to Christ being God.

- The elect angels are dependent upon retaining their state of grace by Christ so they willingly work for God without any hesitation.

Angels Can Be Grieved

According to 1 Corinthians 11:10, Paul warns married women to keep their head veiled at worship, for the sake of the angels. Many attempts have been made to try to give a reasonable interpretation of what Paul meant, but most have failed miserably. Only one attempt has survived a scholarly onslaught. What is it? Paul is calling attention to the fact that the angels of God are present in the assemblies of the church. In these assemblies the angels of God watch what goes on. (See Luke 15:10; Ephesians 3:10; Hebrews 1:14; Psalm 88:1.) Because they are present, they become grieved over anything that disrupts or contradicts the order that God has long ago set for His creation.

Why are the angels of God concerned about this? Because:

- God's angels are concerned with the maintenance of the laws and limits imposed upon God's creation.

- The angels of God are grieved when anything might bring scandal on the Christian name. The married woman's behavior that is contrary to God's set order of creation has and will bring great scandal to the Church.

- The angels of God constantly rejoice in understanding the order of God's creation and become grieved by anything that breaks that order.

- They know what God wants and are grieved when it is not carried out.

- They are always present in the assemblies of the church, and they delight in the genuine carrying out of God's order and the subordination of the ranks of God's servants while they are grieved when anyone violates that order.

Angels Had Their Part in the Temple

The common fact that the angels of God have often appeared in the temple of God is not surprising. Such instances of these occurrences are seen clearly in Scripture. (See Isaiah 6:1–7; Ezekiel 1:4–28; 8:3, 9:6 10:5–7; Luke 1:18–20.) However, what is so surprising to many is the fact that they were involved in the temple.

That the angels had a great involvement in the temple is witnessed by Daniel 4:22, according to the Greek Septuagint. In this passage, Daniel tells Nebuchadnezzar that the reason judgment would fall upon him was due to his pride over those things which pertain to God and to His angels. This was the temple.

The fact that the angels of God were involved in the temple and its workings and would bring judgment upon those who tried to harm it is well attested by history itself. During the reign of Seleucus IV, king of the Syrian empire, Heliodorus the treasurer was sent to seize the treasure found in the Jewish temple. However, Heliodorus failed by divine power. Second Maccabees 3:1–40 tells the story about Heliodorus coming to seize the treasure which had been said to be found in the temple. God came to the rescue of the High Priest, Onias III. All that came into the treasury of the temple were astonished at the power of God and fainted or were sorely afraid. They all beheld a horse with a terrible rider upon it adorned with a very fair covering. The horse ran fiercely and smote Heliodorus with his forefoot. Two other men appeared before Heliodorus in strength, excellent beauty, and comely apparel, and literally beat him. They gave him many stripes on his back. Heliodorus fell down speechless without any hope of life. Some of Heliodorus' friends pleaded with Onias III to pray to God so that he would live. The same two men who beat Heliodorus appeared again. They stood beside Heliodorus and told him that for the sake of Onias III God had granted that his life would be restored. Because of God's intervention, Heliodorus was unable to plunder the temple treasury.

A Plea for the Angels to Be Strengthened

Deuteronomy 32:43 is part of a song of vengeance that Moses sung before the Jewish people. In the last verse, notice from the Greek Septuagint, Moses declares to the angels to give worship to God and to be strengthened in Him because He will avenge the blood of His children the Israelites. Apparently, Moses recognized that many angels were distressed over the state of the Jewish people. On this account, Moses sought to ease the minds of the angels by telling them, through this song, that God had promised that the blood of those Jews already killed would be avenged. How? God would render vengeance and recompense justice to their enemies.

What does Moses mean about pleading that the angels be strengthened in God? Undoubtedly, the Jewish people had suffered so much by their enemies, and God had not yet moved to stop this, that the angels of God had become very grieved about the situation and low in spirit. Moses sought that God would strengthen the angels in spirit and in hope over what He was going to do about this situation.

Angels Laugh

According to the Greek Septuagint, God proclaims to Job that the angels of God laugh at the hippopotamus and serpent. Why do God's angels do this? Studying history itself, there appeared cults worshiping the hippopotamus and serpent. So, to the angels of God, the attempt to worship a creature is so ridiculous that they laugh uncontrollably about it. It was the strangest and craziest thing that they had ever seen.

During Job's time persons were promoting the power of these two animals as proof that they were gods. For this reason, God wanted to show the impotent strength these animals have when compared to Him.

Animal worship was quite common in Egypt. Through this verse God points to animal worship as being so ridiculous that the angels of God laugh at it.

The Greek noun δράκων (thräkōn) found in Job 41:20 is best translated as *serpent* instead of dragon. The serpent is what is intended.

Angels Have Power Over Sight

Power over sight means what? It is a supernatural ability found in both spiritual beings and demons. Demons cannot use it in the physical realm, but only in visions and dreams. All spiritual beings, including God Himself, can use it in visions, dreams, and in the physical realm.

What does this supernatural ability enable them to do? This supernatural ability enables them to change one's perception of how one sees them. How do they do this? They hinder, retain, repress, and control one's eyes or mind so that what one is seeing is not truly reality. Through this ability they can cause another person to see them as they want to be seen and not as they really are. With this knowledge about this ability, angels are recognized as having their own form while being able to cause a person to see them in any form that is acceptable to God's standards. They are not changing from one form to another, but what is changed is how they are seen by a person.

This supernatural ability answers some very puzzling questions about the belief that the human dead appear in dreams and visions. It is not the human dead at all, but it can be angels instead of demons appearing as such. Through this ability, they can cause another person to see them as the human dead. Yet, it is an angel, and not the human dead who are truly seen.

A few examples of this ability are:

- In Acts 16:8–10, a man of Macedonia appears to Paul in a vision. Paul at this time and before this time had not entered Europe, and this vision was a call for Paul to evangelize Europe. The very fact that Paul knew this man was a Macedonian indicates that this man was known by Paul, and Paul had dealings with him before. (See Acts 16:8–10.) However, it was an angel who employed the power over sight and appeared. It was not the angel that changed his form, but it was Paul's perception of what he saw that was changed.

- In Acts 12:7–19, Peter came to the house of Mary and knocked upon the door for the occupants to let him in after the supernatural power of an angel had released him. While the young woman recognized his voice, knew it was Peter, and because of her gladness did not let him in, the other persons in the house did not at first believe that it was Peter who was knocking upon the door. They thought that it was an angel whom the young woman saw as Peter. The belief that angels can change one's perception of what is seen is firmly stated here. The occupants of the house including Mary, the damsel, John Mark, and many others maintain that angels on occasion can be seen as someone else.

- Christ is seen as having this ability after His resurrection. Luke 24:16 maintains that Christ in His human resurrected body physically appeared to two disciples without them recognizing who He was. According to this verse, this occurred by their eyes being affected so that they could not recognize Him in the physical realm. The Greek verb κρατέω (krätĕō) used in Luke 24:16 means that the two disciples were under the power of Christ so that He could influence their eyes and keep them from recognizing Him. He did this by retraining, hindering, or repressing their eyes' normal process of operation. Because of this, the form of what Christ wanted to be seen and recognized as was seen.

- In Deuteronomy 4:15–20, God tells the Jews that He will not appear to them due to their tendencies to become idolaters. God did not appear to the Jews as a male, female, beast of the earth, winged bird that flies above the earth, reptile that creeps on the earth, or fish in the waters. This passage does not at all teach that God is sexless and formless. On the contrary, this passage shows that while God has a real divine form, He did not want the Jews at this time to perceive Him in any manner, including manners that could have been wrought by the power over sight.

- The appearance of Elijah and Moses must be an example of this ability when they appeared before Christ on the Mount of Transfiguration.

- First, as it relates to Moses' appearing, the difficulty stems around the fact that Moses died. If Moses truly appeared here, then Christ was practicing necromancy, which is forbidden. (See Deuteronomy 18:11; Isaiah 8:19; 1 Samuel 28:7–25.) Necromancy is the heathen, ungodly, and abominable practice of trying to communicate with the human dead. The fact that Moses died refutes the common belief that Moses could appear in a vision on the Mount of Transfiguration since that would dictate the practice of necromancy. (See Joshua 1:2; Deuteronomy 32:48; 33:1; 34:5–12.) Spiritualism and those who practice it have found support for their beliefs in Matthew 17:1–8, Mark 9:2–10, and Luke 9:28–36. How? They use these scriptures to try to prove that one can communicate with the human dead.

- Second, as it relates to Elijah appearing, the difficulty arises from the fact that Elijah only has one coming, not two. (See Malachi 4:5.) Elijah is to appear in the Tribulational Period as one witness. (See Revelation 11:3–12; Zechariah 4:11–14; Malachi 4:4–6.) Therefore, if one admits that Elijah appeared on the Mount of Transfiguration, then Elijah could not appear in the last days since he shall only appear once.

- Who were the persons who appeared to Christ if they were not Elijah and Moses? Simply, the two persons were angels using the power over sight to those apostles who saw this. The two angels influenced these apostles' minds to see them as these men. It was not these two angels' forms that changed, but it was the seers' perception of what they saw that was changed. The two angels representing the images of these two men was done to show the approval of Christ from the prophets and the priests.

- In 1 Samuel 28:7–25 and 1 Chronicles 10:13–14, there appears one who resembles the form of Samuel. Who was this? This is known by several points founded upon these verses.

- It is clear from ancient texts and the ancient church that Saul sought after a person who was possessed of a demon.

- It is clear from these texts that Saul did not ask the Lord, but wanted to ask from a demon.

- God would not answer Saul. If God refused to answer Saul, then it is firmly stated that God would never answer him in a way contrary to Scripture.

- The Bible plainly teaches that communications with the human dead are in reality communication with demons imitating the departed. (See Isaiah 8:19; 1 Samuel 28:7–25; 1 Chronicles 10:13–15.)

- It is commanded in many scriptures for people not to traffic with demons or to try to communicate with the human dead. So, God would not allow Samuel to communicate through a witch.

◆ Jesus taught that communicating with living persons on earth is impossible for the human dead. (See Luke 16:26–31.)

◆ It is understood from 1 Samuel 28:7 that Saul sought demonic information.

◆ The woman seeing gods ascending out of the earth in verse 13 of 1 Samuel 28 gives the answer here. These gods are none other than demons.

◆ It is understood from the demon possessing the woman that he went from her and appeared as Samuel and that after that appearance went back into her and began to speak through her in the voice of Samuel. The reason this is so is because the vision was not to Saul, but to a woman.

◆ God was the enemy of Saul, not his friend. (See 1 Samuel 28:6, 16.)

◆ It is attested that Saul and his sons would be with the one speaking through the witch tomorrow. How could this being be Samuel when he was in Paradise and not tormented? The idea here is that the demon said that tomorrow Saul and his sons by their death would be in the underworld with him, which deals with punishment and torment.

◆ How could a woman filled with a demon have power over a saint who is protected by the hand of God? (See John 10:28.)

◆ 2 Samuel 12:23 and Job 10:21 reveal that the human dead cannot come back to appear to humans on earth.

◆ In Zechariah 5:9, two women appear in a vision to Zechariah. Zechariah 5:5–11 concerns the time of the end where the literal Babylon, the city of Babylon, will be completely rebuilt on the same spot as the old city of Babylon. The women represent in this vision two satanic chief angels. These angels of Satan will achieve this rebuilding by their power. Nevertheless, Zechariah

5:5–11 also concerns economical Babylon, political Babylon, and religious Babylon all being revived or rebuilt. Who are these satanic chief angels? First, there is the satanic chief angel of Rome. Second, there is the satanic chief angel over the Syrian empire. The satanic chief angel of Rome will be the real power behind the Roman Empire in its new futuristic form. The satanic chief angel over the Syrian Empire will be over the Syrian division of this new empire initiated by the power of the satanic chief angel of Rome.

♦ Zechariah saw these satanic chief angels as women. However, the satanic chief angels are not women; but the angels have the ability to change a person's perception of what they are seen as. So, they purposely appeared as women by God's orders, not by changing themselves, but by changing Zechariah's perception of what he was seeing. Why? To express the evilness of the thing that was done in that instance. The form of a man or a woman in a vision can be employed for good purposes and evil purposes.

Angels Have the Power of Projection

What does "power of projection" mean? It is a supernatural ability found in both spiritual beings, including God Himself, and demons. Demons cannot use it in the physical realm but only in visions and dreams.

What does this supernatural ability enable them to do? It enables them to project their form and other various kinds of forms upon one's eyes or mind. This supernatural ability is seen in all the passages already given in reference to power over sight. It works in dreams, visions, and in the physical realm.

Angels Have the Power of Manipulation

Power of manipulation is also a supernatural ability found in both spiritual beings, including God Himself, and demons. It enables them to manipulate matter from its original form to another form. This supernatural ability usually concerns things in the physical realm. A clear example of this ability is seen in Exodus 7:11–13. In this passage, it is recorded that the forces of evil, for the sake of the magicians, did not create serpents but changed matter from one form to another. The original forms of matter were rods. They changed all of the matter from rods to serpents. While angels, whether good or evil, and demons can change matter from one form to another form, none can give life to anything. Only God can give life. (See Deuteronomy 32:29; 1 Samuel 2:6; 2 Kings 5:7; Psalm 33:6; Colossians 1:16; James 1:17; Hebrews 1:7; Proverbs 8:22–31; Acts 17:28; Isaiah 45:18.)

The serpents remained lifeless. God breathed life into them. Why? So that He could prove His power over Satan and all the forces of evil. Many other scriptures show God's wonder-working power and its ability to create living creatures at His will. (See Exodus 4:3; 7:10; 7:19–21; 8:5–6; 8:16–17; 8:24, and 10:12–15.)

Angels Come On God's Agenda, Not Their Own

A terrible misconception about the angels of God today is that they will come on their own agenda to a person. This is false. God's angels come to perform the command of the Lord. They do not come for their own reasons, but His alone. This is seen in the life of Daniel and his experiences with angels. No angel who talked with Daniel and no angel who ever appeared to Daniel did these things for their own purpose. They came on the agenda of the Lord. Since they are the representatives of God, they could do nothing but this. This is clearly seen in Daniel 10:19. Gabriel became upset with Daniel for not understanding what he was telling him. Daniel, by not understanding what Gabriel was telling him, was delaying and hindering him from accomplishing the business that God intended to be done. This caused Gabriel to become upset and angry. (See Daniel 10:19.) It is for this reason that Gabriel talked to Daniel so bluntly. Gabriel came to achieve God's business and not to do anything else but that.

So, the angels of God come to achieve God's purpose, and anything that tries to hinder them causes them to be upset and angry. Often when this occurs, they will bring forth judgments. (See Luke 1:18–20.)

Angels Cannot Be Loosed or Bound by a Saint

Another terrible misconception about the angels of God today is the belief that a saint, by using the power of loosing and binding, can loose the angels to work for them or can bind them at will. The problem with this conception is the fact that the power of loosing and binding is not a weapon formed by God to be used against Him. No! It is a weapon formed by God to be used by His saints to fight the onslaughts of Satan and his forces. It cannot be used against God the Father, God the Son, God the Holy Spirit, or the angels of God.

Can saints ask God to loose His angels? Yes! Saints are just asking God to do it. Studying Matthew 16:19, Christ uses the *subjunctive mood* concerning the "power of loosing and binding." What does this mean? Christ by using this mood means that certain things cannot be loosed or bound but are exempted. God the Father, God the Son, God the Holy Spirit, and the angels of God are exempted. The proof is beyond doubt and question. How does this mood show this? It means probability. So, the idea is that whatever is loosed or bound by a saint has only a probability that it will be loosed or bound. This is nothing essentially more than common sense. God being sovereign demands that He could allow nothing else. He is God and not a saint. It is left up to Him whether using the power of loosing and binding will accomplish anything. If not, then the saint would be the master, and God would be the servant.

The proof that the power of loosing and binding is directed only against the powers of Satan and his forces is well attested and confirmed. (See Ephesians 2:6; Colossians 1:13; Luke 10:19; Mark 16:1–18; Ephesians 6:12; Hebrews 2:9; James 4:7; 1 Peter 5:7–8.) All weapons of the saint's warfare have been formed not to be directed against anyone, except Satan and all his forces. (See Ephesians 6:11–19; 2 Corinthians 10:4.)

Angels Can Change Their Size at Will

A common fact that is not known today about angels is the undeniable truth that they can change their size at will. This is not limited just to the angels.

Proof of this is seen when comparing Daniel 12:5–7 with Revelation 10:1–11 and recognizing that the person that appeared in each was Gabriel. In Daniel 12:5–7, Gabriel is seen by Daniel to be the size of a normal man. Nevertheless, in Revelation 10:1–11, John beholds Gabriel as gigantic in size. Gabriel was so large that he could place one foot on the sea and another on the earth. (See Revelation 10:2, 5.) The obvious conclusion is that there are not two different Gabriels, but one Gabriel with the ability to change his size.

This ability is also seen to be possessed by God as well. Isaiah 66:1 and Matthew 5:35 state that the second heaven is God's throne, and the earth is His footstool. Of course, these verses concern God's greatness, but they also express that God can appear in a gigantic size. In Daniel 7:9–10 and Revelation 4:1–5:14, God is also seen to be gigantic in size. Yet, there are many passages in which God is seen to appear as a normal size. (See Isaiah 6:1–7; Daniel 7:9–14; Ezekiel 1:13, 26–28; 8:2; 10:4, 18; 43:4–5; 44:4; Exodus 33:23.) How does one reconcile this contradiction? God possesses the ability to change size at will. It was this ability that allowed God the Word to reduce Himself in size so that He could be placed in the womb of Mary and unite Himself with an ovum of Mary. If God the Word did not have this ability, the incarnation could not have been accomplished at all. Therefore, God the Word did this miracle by transforming Himself to the similar size of an ovum so that He and one of Mary's ova could be united under the direct ministry of the Holy Spirit. It was the ovum of Mary that gave God the Word a human body. The whole Godhead created the human soul and spirit that Christ received at conception. (See Isaiah 42:5; 57:16; Zechariah 12:1; Hebrews 12:9.) Certain attributes of the human soul and spirit of Christ were created by the whole Godhead while the rest were inherited through Mary, though not an exact duplicate of, but different in degree.

Angels Are Organized into Six Orders

In scripture, the orders of God's angels are only truly known. Scriptures do tell us the orders of God's angels by mentioning thrones, dominions, authorities, powers, and principalities as orders of God's angels. (See Ephesians 1:21; Colossians 1:16.) By Ephesians 1:21, and other scriptures, it can easily be concluded that the apostles and the early Christians only believed in six orders. This is seen in that five names are designated as orders in these scriptures: thrones, dominions, authorities, powers, and principalities. The sixth name is "angel." When angel is used with these five other names, it only has reference to the common angels. Apart from these names, the name *angel* has reference to all those spiritual beings that God both created and organized into six orders. So, any spiritual being from any of these six orders is an angel, except the spiritual horses.

The apostles and the early church apparently understood what order of God's angels is meant by each designation. This was understood by defining what is meant by each designation:

- The term *thrones* are those angels who sit upon thrones, rule over God's kingdom on His behalf, are the first order, and are termed the seats of angelic power instigated by God.

- The term *dominions* are those angels who rule for the thrones. They are the second order and are termed the lords of angelic power. They also rule over galaxies controlled by the kingdom of God.

- The term *authorities* are angels whom the dominions invest with imperial responsibility. They are the third order and are termed those who exercise the rule of the angelic Lords by ruling over the solar systems controlled by the kingdom of God.

- The term *powers* are angels who exercise supremacy of the authorities' power. They are the fourth order and are those who go throughout the kingdom of God as scouts and invade Satan's kingdom as spies receiving and finding information. They also help enforce God's law and are reserve fighters in battles and wars.

- The term *principalities* are angels who govern the common angels. They are the fifth order and are those who rule and report to the powers on the affairs of the places that they rule over.

- The term *angels* are those angels whom the principalities govern and are the last order.

To the apostles and the early Christians, the conclusion from these six designations was obvious. They concluded that the Seraphim are referred to by thrones, the Cherubim are referred to by dominions, the Ofannim—wheel angels—are referred to by authorities, the angels that ride spiritual horses and drive spiritual horse-chariots are referred to by powers, the chief angels are referred to by principalities, and common angels are referred to simply as angels.

An early Christian work entitled *The Pastor of Hermas*, written in the second century, held the belief that there are only six orders of God's angels. Hermas sees six young men in a vision. According to the interpretation of the young men given in the vision, the young men symbolize the six orders of God's angels.[5] Many have concluded that although Ezekiel 9:2 literally has reference to six Cherubim, the six young men symbolically represent the six orders of God's angels.

Why are the six orders of God's angels known as *thrones, dominions, authorities, powers, principalities*, and *angels*? These terms indicate that God's kingdom is organized, and each order is limited in what it has control over. These terms are a sign of the angels' limitation. Further, these names depict different positions of power that each order has and a succession of orders one after the other. To see that the angels of God are found in orders is only logical. As the universe has been set in order, so have the angels of God. They have been set in orders and groups in their orders according to the order found in the universe. The groups are also based upon certain facts interwoven throughout the passages that have reference to angels.

Notes

CHAPTER 1
THE ORDERS OF GOD'S ANGELS: THE SERAPHIM

1. *Antiquities of the Jews* 9.10.4.
2. Maimonides, *The Code of Maimonides*, 8: 259, 262, 393, 397, 401; Lightfoot, John B. *The Works of John Lightfoot*, 1:898, 950–951.
3. Middoth, 14.

CHAPTER 2
THE ORDERS OF GOD'S ANGELS: THE CHERUBIM

1. Irenæus, *Against Heresies*, 5:35.2 (1:565).

CHAPTER 3
THE ORDERS OF GOD'S ANGELS: THE OFANNIM

1. *Rosh Hashanah*, 106; *Hagigah*, 72–80.

CHAPTER 4
THE OTHER ORDERS OF GOD'S ANGELS

1. *Yoma*, 374.
2. *Makkoth*, 80.

CHAPTER 5
ANGELIC ATTRIBUTES COMMONLY KNOWN

1. Irenæus, *Against Heresies*, 5.5:1–3 (1:530–531); Augustine, *On Forgiveness of Sins*, and *Baptism*, 1.3 (1.5:16); Ambrose, *On the Christian Faith*, 4.1:1–14 (2.10:263).
2. Hermas, *The Pastor of Hermas*, 2.5.1 (2:23).
3. Tertullian, *Of Patience*, 6 (3:711).
4. Basil, *The Hexaemeron*, 1:5–8 (2.8.54–56); Gregory of Nyssa, *The Hexaemeron*, 68–72 (2.5:8–11); Augustine, *De. Gen. Contra Manich* L. 2.c.3; Augustine, *De. Gen. Lit.* L.1.c.2.; *De. Gen. Ad. Lit.* L.5.C.3.

CHAPTER 6
ANGELIC ATTRIBUTES LESS KNOWN

1. Josephus, *Wars of the Jews*, 7:6.3; *1 Enoch* 15:8–11; *1 Enoch* 16:1; *Jubilees* 10:5–11.

2. *Kalonymos Ben Kalonymos, Iggeret Baale Hayyim*; *Ancient Israel, Myths and Legends*, 75; *The Midrash Rabbah*, 1:89; 3: 548; *Book of Jasher*; *Genesis Targum* 1:2; *Zohar*, Genesis 2:4–6.

3. Hesiod, *Works and Days*, 109–126.

4. Justin Martyr, *The First Apology of Justin*, 18 (1:169); Ignatius, *Epistle to the Smyrnæans* 2 (1:87); Irenæus, *Against Heresies* 4:36 (1:516); Athenagoras, *A Plea for Christians*, 24–25 (2:141–142); Tertullian, *Apology*, 23; Origen, *Origen Against Celsus*, 8.55; Arnobius, *The Seven Books of Arnobius Against the Heathen*, 1.45; John Chrysostom, *Commentary on the Epistle of St. Paul to the Galatians*, 5.

5. Edersheim, *The Life and Times of Jesus the Messiah*, 1:142.

6. Irenæus, *Against Heresies*, 1:28; 3:23 (1:353; 1:455–458).

7. Anathemas, *Against Origen* 4; Fragment from *Origen de Principiis*.

8. Wuest, *Word Studies in the Greek New Testament*, 1:104.

9. Clement of Alexandria, *The Instructor*, 2:13 (2:267); *Stromata*, 6:16.4 (2:513); Origen, *De Principiis*, 2.9:1–2 (4:290), 3.5:3 (4:341–342); Hippolytus, *Fragments From Commentaries*, 4 (5:197); Origen, *Commentary in Genesis*, 145; Procopius of Gaza, *Commentary in Genesis*, 35–43.

10. Gromacki, Robert G. *The Virgin Birth, Doctrine of Deity*, 97; Tertullian, *On the Flesh of Christ*, 23.

11. Irenæus, op. cit., 2.8.6 (1:386).

12. Hagigah, 101–102.

13. Ignatius, *The Epistle to the Smyrenæans*, 2, 3 (1: 87).

14. Augustine, *Enchiridion*, 59 (1.3:256).

15. Ibid., *The City of God*, 15.23 (1.2:303).

16. Tertullian, *Against Marcion*, 3.9 (3:328–329).

17. Ibid., *On the Flesh of Christ*, 3 (3:523).

18. Ibid., 6 (3:527).

19. John Cassian, *First Conference of Abbot Serenus*, 13 (2.11:366–367).

20. Origen, *De Principiis*, 2.9:3 (4:290).

21. *Wars*, 2.8.7.

22. *Shabbath*, 418.
23. *Hagigah*, 104.
24. *Revelation of John*, (8:583).

CHAPTER 7
ANGELIC WORKS COMMONLY KNOWN

1. *Antiquities of the Jews* 15.5.3.

CHAPTER 8
ANGELIC WORKS LESS KNOWN

1. *The Midrash Rabbah*, 3:411; 2:629; 2:711; 9:326.
2. Augustine, *On the Trinity*, 3.11:25–27 (13:67).
3. Basil, *On the Spirit*, 13:30 (2.8:19).
4. Augustine, *On the Psalm*, 97.10 (2.8:477).

CHAPTER 10
OTHER ANGELIC FACTS LESS KNOWN

1. Ignatius *Epistle to the Ephesians*, 19 (1:57).
2. Ignatius, *Epistle to the Philippians*, 9 (1:118).
3. Ibid., 4 (1:117).
4. Augustine, *Enchiridion*, 27–28 (3:246–247).
5. 1: 4–6 (2:14).

For more information concerning Dr. Roberts, his mother, their schedule of events, their ministry and donations to that ministry, please contact:

True Light Ministries
P.O. Box 28538
Jacksonville, FL 32218
A Non-Profit and Tax-Exempt Organization
Cell: 904-472-7786
Fax: 904-751-0304
truelightministries.org

For I shall bring forth truth out of darkness for the sake of my people.